ONCE UPON A TIME

Dear Jammy & Jenna,
May you find
your joy
in Jesus.
Warmly,
✝ Jody

James 1:2-4

ONCE UPON A TIME

JODY CAPEHART

VICTOR BOOKS

A DIVISION OF SCRIPTURE PRESS PUBLICATIONS INC.
USA CANADA ENGLAND

Unless otherwise noted, all Scripture references are from the *Holy Bible, New International Version*®. Copyright © 1973, 1978, 1984 by International Bible Society. Used by permission of Zondervan Publishing House. All rights reserved; other references are from *The Living Bible* (TLB), © 1971, Tyndale House Publishers, Wheaton, IL 60189. Used by permission.

Editors: Mary Sytsma and Barbara Williams
Cover Design: Grace K. Chan Mallette
Cover Illustration: Chuck Slack

Library of Congress Cataloging-in-Publication Data

Capehart, Jody.
    Once upon a time / Jody Capehart.
      p.   cm.
    1. Mothers—United States—Religious life.
    2. Capehart, Jody.
   3. Mothers—United States—Biography.
    I. Title.
  BV4847.C37   1994
248.8'431'092—dc20
[B]   94-13405
                                          CIP

---

1 2 3 4 5 6 7 8 9 10 Printing/Year 98 97 96 95 94

Dedication

To the many people
whom God has woven
into the tapestry
of my life to make it
what He would have it
to be for His purpose.
To our Lord and Savior,
Jesus Christ, who by
His love and grace,
makes all things new.
"Therefore, if anyone
is in Christ, he is
a new creation,
the old has gone,
the new has come!"
(2 Cor. 5:17)

Contents

Acknowledgments

There are many dear people who made this book possible and I wish to express my sincere appreciation to you and I wish we could list each of you here.

First of all, to such faithful friends as Jean Conner who urged me over the years to "share my story in order to be an encouragement to others."

To Don Geiger who was my pastor when I was a new Christian and who inspired me to "put my past behind me as Saul did and to go forward to serve Jesus Christ as Paul did." It was through Don ministering to me that I began to serve in a teaching ministry in a Bible church and I am deeply grateful for his wisdom and direction.

To Mark Sweeney, vice president and publisher of Victor Books, who asked me to write this book and gave me permission to simply "be myself."

To all of you who prayed when I realized that writing this book brought up some old pain and I found I got emotionally stuck and couldn't "get funny" while staring at my computer.

To Sandi Glahn who, over a meeting to discuss going to Russia to teach, helped me to find the humor in my past once again. Through Sandi allowing me to tell my stories and laughing, which encouraged me to "get funny," the book began to get new life. Then, through Sandi patiently transcribing and reworking those many audiotapes with me, came the final manuscript. Sandi also provided some of the spiritual applications for the chapters.

To Sue Bohlin, who has provided much encouragement and prayer for this project, as well as some of the spiritual applications.

To Greg Clouse and Barbara Williams who were ideal editors to work with during this project.

To my family who provided love, acceptance, and humor which became the heart of this book.

Introduction

Once upon a time there was a little girl who became a Christian at age five, met her husband at Bible College, and spaced her 2.3 children at perfect intervals. She had a manicured lawn with real flowers, wore designer clothes on her perky figure, got her fake nails manicured weekly, led her maid to Christ, and rose cheerfully at 4 A.M. to have her quiet time before going to the club to work out. After low-impact aerobicizing, she returned to gently awaken her husband, for whom she had prepared a perfectly healthy breakfast on prewarmed china plates. She said meaningful things to her children before sending them off to private school in outfits she had made herself. (And they carried brightly decorated lunch bags in which she had tucked Scripture verses.) Then she fed their 2.3 pets, balanced the checkbook to the penny, and went off to teach other women how they too could lead the "Normal Christian Life." Everyone called her a Proverbs 31 woman. And she and her family lived happily ever after serving the Lord.

That's what I would like to tell you is the story of my life. But that would be a fairy tale.

The honest version would sound more like this.

Once upon a time there was an ugly duckling child who played house and aspired to have twelve children someday—until she grew up and her doctor told her she probably would never be able to conceive. As an adult, she longed to be a teacher, but when she grew up, her state had a surplus of teachers. She longed to be a perfect wife and mother, but in her twenties she strayed from her upbringing. When she did finally come to know the Lord and became a wife and mother, she longed for the "Normal Christian Life." But in reality, she occasionally served her family Ragu instead of making spaghetti sauce from scratch. She sometimes went to bed without removing her eye makeup and even left the water running while brushing her teeth, despite warnings from her ecologically minded family. And yes, she even hid stashes of candy bars and inducted herself into the Weight Watchers' Hall of Shame.

Could God really use someone such as she? Could it be that even she could have a ministry? Yes, because God had a plan for her life. He was more interested in her *availability* than her *ability*.

Cherished
Childhood

*W*as I a beautiful baby? Well, let's just say when Gerber's talent scouts saw me, they gasped and ran the other way with their contract. My mother still hasn't accepted this reality — so please don't tell her.

I had crossed eyes; I had to wear hideous glasses. And I had to have an operation so I could breathe. Before that, my mouth hung open in a desperate effort to suck in oxygen. When friends look at my childhood pictures, they say, "I didn't know you had a retarded sister."

"That was me."

"Oh. . . ."

Aside from being somewhat strange looking, I had a fairly normal childhood — if you can call being one of seven siblings normal. We lived in a small town in Minnesota. My daddy ran a gas station, so we never had much money. But we felt rich in things that mattered: family, love, a bazillion critters and a television.

My brothers frequently caught frogs and impounded them in peanut butter jars. While they slept, I would often sneak down and remove the lids. Please don't tell my brothers — they still don't know I did that. Well, maybe they do. Maybe that's why they would chase me, hold me down, and shove snakes and frogs down my pants.

Sometimes my brothers got the best of me. Once as we were horsing around at the lake, I started to get out of the water when I felt something move under my swimming suit. As I put my hand down, I felt a sea monster in my pants. I did what any brave young heroine would do — I screamed at the top of my lungs and waved my arms uncontrollably. My father, who was no swimmer, jumped in, clothes and all, to deliver his distressed daughter. He managed to fish the terrified frog out of my swimsuit — though I was squirming more than it was.

I have never "bonded" well with reptiles — especially the snakes that lurked underneath my bed. At night, I would stare wide-eyed at the ceiling trying to suppress the sensation coming from my expanding bladder, terrified the snakes would devour me if my feet hit the hardwood. When I reached the point of desperation, I would bolt from the bed and run to the bathroom.

When I'd finished taking care of business, I'd turn on the light and slowly pull up my bedspread to peek under the bed. "OK . . . whew! . . . no snakes . . ." Yet as soon as I climbed back into bed, I begin to worry again about those ugly reptiles.

I never saw them, but I know they were there.

I loved all my other creatures, and I always let my animals sleep with me. On Easter one year, I woke up to discover my cat had kittens in my baby bed, which I thought was cool, and so did my Mom. I used to dress up my dogs in doll clothes and pretend they were babies. The only things I loved more than animals were babies.

I saw one key advantage of being the only girl with five brothers (the first ten years of my life): I got to have my own bedroom. So I became a loner. I could play for hours in my room, where I spent the better part of each day doing what healthy girls of any age do — rearranging furniture. I continually tried to figure out the best way to divide the room into two sections. One was my playhouse; the other, my schoolhouse.

I spent my childhood pretending I was a mom and a teacher.

Sometimes I would go with my mother to take my older brother to school. I noticed the first-grade teacher wore white, terry cloth slippers. Too young to understand that she had broken her foot during the summer, I got the idea that "Real Teachers Wear Terry Cloth Slippers." So whenever I played school, I included as essential to my uniform some white terry cloth slippers. In my mind, this was as integral to being a teacher as going to teachers college.

In the morning I rose, dressed, fed all 100,000 dolls, and carried them over to the playschool. These fantasy children were silent, obedient, in fact, perfect—exactly what my real children would, of course, someday be.

I do cherish my childhood. It is so much a part of who and what I am today. It wasn't perfect, but it was warm and wonderful. My parents definitely had their priorities centered on us kids. My extended family provided much of the enrichment as well. My mom's family provided lots of fun times at the lake and special trips. My father's family provided time on the farm riding the tractor and playing with the animals.

Our home was the meeting place for the entire neighborhood. We had kids in the house, playing in the yard, and in the basement. Our house was on a hill and so, during the sledding season, it was certainly the focal point for everyone.

But the neatest thing my parents provided for us kids was a bus. They didn't have much money, but we never knew it. They bought an overturned school bus and converted it into a home for us to go camping with in the summer. Yes, we slept all of us in the bus. It was wall-to-wall people, but we didn't care. We loved it! This is the richest memory all of us kids have. Talk about closeness . . . we had it!

When I was in junior high, they moved us to a farm. It was an old, run-down farm that they spent a year cleaning and fixing up. I was peaking on the junior high social scene and did not welcome it at first. But the beauty of having quiet, and orchards and rolling hills to run and play in became a real blessing.

I spent most of my teenage years baby-sitting, including baby-sitting for my younger siblings, devoting hours to perfecting the art. When I baby-sat for other people, I would always take a bag of activities to do with the children. I took this vocation very seriously and soon found myself in demand. I often had between ten and twenty calls to baby-sit on one night. When parents came home, they found the house spotless, their children well cared for, dishes done, and clothes washed and folded.

Just like all the baby-sitters I hire today for my own kids. NOT.

I deeply appreciate the fact that my parents, Chet and Donna Kvanli, have always been there for me. They believed in me and let me pursue my dreams. I am abundantly blessed.

Jesus loves ugly ducklings. He has to. He made so many of us. It must give Him a divine thrill to create such beauty in people — so exquisitely disguised.

Growing up ugly or handicapped or disfigured *hurts*. Yet, just like the little ugly duckling in the fairy tale, physical ugliness is only temporary. It's a matter of perspective and time. Whether you grow out of it on earth or have to wait for your new body in heaven, sometimes it's only a matter of how people perceive beauty. Making friends with humble, accepting people can make a big difference in one's self-image.

One of the most handsome, powerful, charismatic men in history knew what it was like to be an ugly duckling. Dismissed by his father as young and inconsequential, David nonetheless was a "beautiful swan" that no one but God could see. When He told Samuel to anoint David as Israel's next king, God told the prophet, "The Lord does not look at the things man looks at. Man looks at the outward appearance, but the Lord looks at the heart" (1 Sam. 16:7).

Ugly ducklings can have the priceless satisfaction of knowing that inner beauty, potential or real, is just as obvious to God as the . . . zits on our faces.

When I Grow Up, I'm Goin' to Marry Daddy

One day my mother presented me with some items for dress-up play—a black skirt, a red sweater, and some old Avon samples. Little did she realize this would be a life-transforming experience for me.

I ascended to my room and decked myself out in my new threads. Then I slipped my tiny feet into her high heels and outlined the curves on my lips with the Avon lipstick samples. Instinctively I knew to "stuff" the red sweater. I loved the look, so this outfit became a permanent addition to my play.

At dinnertime, I would usually wipe off the lipstick and unstuff the sweater. But one particular evening as I looked at myself, I thought, "Ya know, I look pretty gooood." As little girls often do, I thought, "I want Daddy to see me. Because if he saw me, he would want to marry me instead of Mom, who's always pregnant, anyhow. . . ."

I was sure my father would take one look, fall to his knees to propose, and we'd walk off into the sunset.

When I entered the room looking like Dolly Parton's twin, my older brother nearly fell off his chair convulsing with laughter. My parents threatened to send him to a pre-teen penitentiary.

My dad smiled, which I took as a smile of passion for me. In reality, he was trying hard to choke back a roar. He glanced at my mother, who spoke in controlled tones and suppressed the urge to die on the floor.

It took awhile for me to realize I had not set my father's heart ablaze with this new look. In fact, it's safe to say I probably provided him with weeks of amusement.

One of the joys of parenthood is that as my children go through stages I went through, I can smile (or sometimes cringe) as their experiences evoke images from my own past. No wonder people often say the strictest father is the one who lived in the fast lane.

I believe every little girl and boy has a right to enjoy that temporal love affair with their opposite parent. When I see my daughter come downstairs trying to look enticing for her father, I remember those feelings all too well.

But, in this life at least, all good things must come to an end.

My son, Christopher told me sorrowfully one night, "Mommy, for years I dreamed of growing up and marrying you, but I just realized something. By the time I'm ready to marry, you're going to be very, very old, and I'm not sure it would work."

"When I was a child, I talked like a child, I thought like a child, I reasoned like a child. When I became a man, I put childish ways behind me" (1 Cor. 13:11).

It's wholly appropriate for children to do childish things, even (and especially) when they're imitating others. Alarms should go off when we see children growing up too soon and assuming, not merely imitating, adult behavior.

But just as alarming is the adult who hasn't put childish ways behind him or her. Temper tantrums belong to pre-schoolers, not to people driving two-ton automobiles at seventy-five miles per hour. And what about the adult who refuses to delay self-gratification? What about the grown-up who has fantasy relationships with someone else's spouse?

The Lord is the ultimate adult, and He can help us grow up in those areas where we haven't. All we need to do is ask.

Are Brothers
a Bother?

I have the distinction of being my parents' first-born. My father brought two children into his marriage with my mother. His son, Alan, lived with us while Alan's sister, Bonnie, lived in California. After I was born, a boy followed once every year for four years. So, in essence, I had five brothers.

How did I handle it? First, I learned to entertain myself alone in my room. I did *not* learn to do sports so I could play with them, but I did learn to hold my own in a family full of people I felt convinced suffered from "testosterone poisoning." While I made no effort to appreciate snakes, frogs, and other reptiles, I did learn to cut deals. For example, I played cops and robbers for thirty minutes in exchange for equal time playing house. And I discovered I got better results from them if I scratched their backs instead of using the "weaker vessel" approach. I began to understand the warped humor shoveled out by the male of the species, and I managed to dish some of it back. All in all, living with all these guys gave me the best possible preparation to serve on a predominantly (all but me) male staff.

Today I love my brothers and feel very proud of them.

Alan has a Ph.D. in statistics and is a professor at a university as well as writing statistics textbooks and serving as a business consultant. He has always been there for me and is a wonderful help with computers and research. Joel is a physician's assistant in a clinic and is an invaluable help with my 4,300 medical maladies. (This week I cracked a couple of ribs. . . .) Joel also worked with me for a couple of years. Kevin works in surgery as a nurse in Rochester Mayo Clinic and Hospital. Kevin has taught me much about the natural life through his passion for outdoor living. Kerry is a missionary in Albania and we are closely bonded with our mutual passion for serving the Lord. Jon died and, had he lived, with all of his needs, he would have perfected my love for those requiring special education. I enjoy a unique bond with each of my brothers and feel grateful for what each contributes to my life.

Are they a bother? Not now. But as a child, when I begged the doctor to put a girl in Mommy's tummy instead of all these stupid boys, I would have said yes.

Aren't you glad God doesn't always give us what we want? During the times of the Prophet Samuel, the Children of Israel asked for a king. Up to that time, God Himself had served as their ruler. But like Americans who want satellite dishes and recreational vehicles just like their neighbors, the Israelites wanted a king like all the other nations had. Samuel told the Lord about it, and God answered, "It is not you they have rejected, but they have rejected Me as their king." Then He instructed Samuel to tell them what a king would require—their sons as horsemen and chariot drivers, their daughters as cooks and bakers, and the best of their servants and produce.

How did the people respond? "We want a king over us. Then we will be like all the other nations, with a king to lead us and to go out before us and to fight our battles" (1 Sam. 8:19-20). God wanted to give them His best but, because they insisted, He gave them what they wanted.

How many times have you looked back and given thanks that God refrained from doing what you asked? Are you struggling over unanswered prayer today? Consider that perhaps the delay has come about because God loves you too much to give you what you want.

Photos
and
Other
Phobias

I believe learning challenges find as their root a
degree of hypersensory acuity. I invite you to
simply accept my hypothesis for now. When in a
social situation, I act hyper. My hypersensory
acuity manifests itself in my need to take photos.
Because I suffer from sensory overload, and because I am
very people-responsive, I absorb everyone's feelings and
have trouble sorting them out. So I have to tune out some of
the incoming data. Since I learn visually, I block the visual
avenue to keep myself from overload. How? I take pictures,
then I go back and look at them when I am not in a state of
hypersensory acuity. Only when I am alone can I absorb the
memories. My husband says I was born with a camera cord
rather than an umbilical cord. Needless to say, I have found
no one who agrees with my hypothesis — not that I have
asked anyone. Have you noticed that no "Photo Phobia"
organization exists for Kodak addicts?

I had never met anyone like me in this way, either. So
imagine my surprise when I met my half-sister for the first
time at age twenty-two. Bonnie grew up in California; my
parents raised me in Minnesota. At our first meeting, our

cameras clicked as fast as Fred Astaire's tap shoes. We bonded instantly.

As the years progressed, we began to see each other frequently. Our common denominators (idiosyncrasies?) constantly amazed us. Even identical twins raised in the same environment could not be more similar. We both exhibited these traits, to name just a few:

1. We both have camera addictions—we're total photo freaks.
2. We both married pastors' sons.
3. We both love education and have served as school principals.
4. We both crave neatness and have been known to make the beds when our husbands arose to go to the bathroom.
5. We both have a crazy sense of humor and laugh ourselves sick.
6. We both think eating chocolate is one way to gain favor with God.
7. We both hyperventilate if we open a drawer and find it still in the "perfect" order in which we left it.
8. We both know we are not neurotic; we have simply redefined "normal."
9. We both feel things deeply, including our stress; we both suffer from migraine headaches.
10. We both work harder than anyone expects or asks.

This last similarity takes us back to my beginning observation—not only do I take in a lot; I also do a lot. This combination can be brutal. I think it was either Moses or Charlton Heston who said, "I have too much to do." Sometimes our lives reach "overload." Like washing machines when we fill them too full, our overcrowded lives can make us go berserk until we rearrange a few things. As Lord Moran wrote in *The Anatomy of Courage*, "[People] of good will saddled with the fate of others need great courage to be idle when only rest can clear their fuddled wits."

I see my sister about once a year. We try to cram twelve

months' worth of events into one weekend of nonstop talking and (yes, did I mention it?) looking at each other's photo albums. Right now we are contemplating making a joint investment — purchasing stock in Kodak.

Summer of '68

Rewind back to the summer of '68. For me, it meant senior year. Prom. Graduation. Today we do sit-ups, but back then we held sit-ins.

In those days, people my age chanted, "Make love, not war," and dedicated themselves to Democratic Party causes. We openly rebelled against our parents, the "establishment," who sported "Nixon's the One" buttons.

That summer I did what all truly feminine women of that time did — I wore patched jeans and pumped gas. I also loved Bobby Kennedy. The night of the California primary, my friends and I planned how we would solve the world's problems — starting tomorrow. It took us into the wee hours of the night (Congress should be so quick). So the next morning, when I arose to get to work by seven, I felt like a cat that had been run over by a freight train.

In my zombied state, I stopped to revive myself by glancing at my copy of LIFE magazine, which featured (sigh) Bobby Kennedy on the cover. The radio played softly in my room, and periodically I heard the announcer say, "Kennedy." I smiled, thinking of the Utopia America would know

now that Bobby had won the primary.

When I arrived at work, my boss said, "Well, they finally got him."

"What do you mean?"

"They got Bobby."

"You mean he won the primary?"

"No. He's dead."

Complete shock swept over me. Layers of my young idealism peeled off me like a banana skin in those seconds. I walked off the job, which I'd never done before or since. Then I went back home and staggered into my bedroom.

I'm compulsively neat. So I expressed my rage by doing the only logical thing—I grabbed each of my drawers and dumped their contents into the center of my room. Then I went to my closet and threw the rest of my clothes on the pile. I suppressed the urge to start a bonfire.

Finally I climbed into bed, pulled the covers over my head, and laid there in my mummified state for days. I could only cry. I told God I did not want to live in a world that would kill Bobby Kennedy. He did not let me die, so it seemed to me there could be only one sane response for a semi-religious person like me to have toward this insanity: I'd become a nun and go to Africa as a missionary.

A part of me died when Bobby Kennedy died—a little piece of my idealism.

And I became a Republican.

Was it wrong for me to feel such intense emotions about a senseless murder? I don't think so. Sometimes we get the incorrect notion that it's bad for us to let ourselves feel really awful. Asaph, who wrote several psalms, let his frustration over the prosperity of the wicked take him close to the point of stumbling. He said, "My feet had *almost* slipped" (italics mine). Yet when he describes himself in this state, he says to God, "I was a brute beast before You." What does a beast act like? I picture a snorting bull ready to charge—or perhaps its human equivalent—a two-year-old throwing a tantrum. Whatever it means, it isn't positive. He continues, "Yet I am always with You; You hold me back by my right hand. You guide me with Your counsel, and afterward You will take me into glory" (Ps. 73:23-24). Even though Asaph said he'd acted like a beast before God, he hadn't stumbled. Asaph was right in feeling upset that the wicked prosper — but he needed to stop himself — and he did — before it led him to bitterness.

The Son of God felt angry when money-changers ripped off worshipers in the temple. David felt outraged when he learned that his son had committed rape. Paul reassures his readers by telling them that God will execute vengeance. Why would this have encouraged them? Because it's good to love justice. The murder of the innocent *should* make us outraged and grief-stricken. It's right to want evil actions to bring consequences. In a world filled with incest and drunk drivers, our longing for wrongs to be made right will cause us to feel really bad sometimes as we stare in disbelief at the injustice around us.

Perhaps someone has deeply wronged you, and you feel a lot of negative emotions about it. That's OK. Yet instead of reaching the point of bitterness, offer your negative emotions to God as a sacrifice, trusting that He is in ultimate control. Remember, the story isn't yet finished. He sees all, works all things for good, and will execute swift and furious justice on behalf of His children in due time.

Basking in My Basement

*D*uring my first year of college, my parents let me move into their basement. They set me up with a little apartment complete with refrigerator, stove, and living area. I wouldn't have felt happier in Buckingham Palace.

I lived every college student's dream — security and freedom, rent-free! When I needed my family, I could join them. I could make dinner for myself, but when I wanted a home-cooked meal, I could ascend into Mom and Dad's world. Also, I was a convenient built-in baby-sitter for them, so it was a "win-win" situation for everyone.

As I began to date more, I developed a "manhood test." Like every other college student in those days, I decorated my walls with posters. In one, a mother nursed her baby in the woods. In the other, two naked babies — one black and one white — sat next to each other. These I used as barometers of male maturity. If a guy came in and gawked or acted offended, I crossed him off my list. If he said, "Wow, that's beautiful," I pursued him.

When the Vietnam protests broke out and campuses across America became arenas for riots, my heart broke. Students rebelled by skipping class, and I became frustrated. Sometimes I was the only student who showed up for class. I had come to get an education, and I wanted to prepare for my future.

The administration shut down our college at midterm, saying everyone would receive the grade he or she had earned at that time. I didn't want the grade—I wanted the education and experience. I remember writing in my journal how painful it felt to watch students jeopardize their futures over issues they didn't understand. But then, they still believed fighting could make a difference. I told myself, "They still have their idealism," thinking I had lost most of mine. But I still had plenty.

I finally seriously dated a man whom I thought I would marry. He alone seemed to understand my dream to have six biological children, and six adopted biracial children. In the middle of our romance, he took a job at the University of Hawaii. Love, leis, and hula dancing sounded good to me, so I decided to follow him to the islands, assuming we would eventually walk off into the Waikiki sunset together as man and wife. I packed my apartment full of stuff and quit my job. Once I had everything in boxes ready to go, he called to break up with me.

I felt devastated and numb. I found new depths of pain, sorrow, and sadness every day. I thought I'd "bottomed out" on hurt, only to discover a new floor to which I hadn't previously fallen.

As the world celebrated Christmas, I mourned my lost love. When my brother, Al, came home from Texas for the holidays, he announced that his marriage had just ended. What a pair we made in our misery. During those holidays, Al and I decided I should move to the South and live with him. Why not . . . I'd already packed. So off we went.

Living in a basement was an apt metaphor for the painful relationships I experienced during this time. Most basements seem like cold, uninviting, second-rate places that never approach the comfortable kind of living space upstairs in the "real" house. (I say "usually" because my basement was an exception—it was warm and wonderful.)

The break-up with my "Hawaii honey" plunged me into such severe feelings of rejection that I kept finding new, deeper emotional basements. More than merely the loss of love, this meant the loss of a dream as well. The sorrow kept carving deeper and deeper caverns in my soul. But as I look back at the pain and rejection that characterized this relationship, and as I think of the other kinds of emotional basements we experience, I remind myself of the Lord's simple promise: "Never will I leave you; never will I forsake you" (Heb. 13:5). God makes the load of our pain bearable by carrying it for us. We can endure rejection by another person, even one we love and trust completely, if we can know we are accepted by God and that God has sworn to us His unfailing love and presence. After all, a basement is just another part of the house when the God of all comfort dwells there with us.

Big D
with
Big Al

*H*ere was the small town MinneSNOWta girl living in the big city with her big brother. Unloading the car that December without a coat, books, scarf, and gloves seemed like Utopia to me. My relationship with the college professor had been VERY serious. We shared philosophy, poetry, and music. But I was never silly around him. With Al, I laughed constantly. I was discovering the polarities of my nature. On one hand, I am a serious, sensitive person who craves solitude. Most people do not know that about me because my people-self is so outgoing, and terribly silly. I was learning more about who I was and wasn't every day.

Al and I learned together that being silly wouldn't take away our grief, but it sure doesn't hurt. We got along so famously and had so much fun that people wondered if we really were siblings. We would go to the grocery store, and he would get me laughing so hard I would have to sit down in the aisle. When I would regain my composure, I would look up only to discover he had left me there looking like an idiot, while he was nowhere in sight.

He let me sleep on the couch, which was plenty fair, since

I wasn't paying any rent. I told him I would happily throw in home-cooked meals, and a back scratch to boot. I got a job as a waitress, which only reinforced my intense desire to be educated and be a teacher.

To relieve the monotony of my job, Al and I tried to find ways to add excitement. Though I was not personally fulfilled by being a waitress, I learned to put a smile on my face and demonstrate a good attitude. I discovered that, if nothing else, I made better tips that way.

One day the restaurant management announced a new policy — waitresses had to wear hair nets, support hose, and orthopedic shoes. Agreeing to that seemed like signing a contract for lifelong celibacy, but considering what I'd been through, that didn't seem like such a bad option. So I went all out — I bought support hose with the seam up the back. Then I found a hair net with the big hole in the front that REALLY looked like a hair net. Nothing delicate about it — it was the kind Ruth Buzzi used to wear on "Laugh-In."

Al would tell people at his work that he'd met this really weird waitress and talk a gang into coming to see me for a little entertainment. When he brought his friends to see me, we pretended we didn't know each other. I always lived up to his descriptions of me — I can do "blonde, dumb, and weird" with ease. We did this for months before he eventually confessed to the guys at work the true identity of that "poor, pitiful waitress."

In those days, women with beehive hairdos graced the covers of most fashion magazines. In anticipation of my first date in Dallas, I decided I *had* to have one of those hip hairstyles. One afternoon, I'd gone directly from the morning shift to have my hair done. When I got home, I fulfilled my responsibilities as Al's housekeeper and took out the trash. But I accidentally tossed the garbage, container and all, into the dumpster. I leaned over to retrieve the garbage can, but I couldn't reach it. In the process, my glasses slid off my face into the gunk.

So I went back to our apartment and got a chair. I carried it down to the dumpster and stood on it, leaning over and reaching as far as I could to retrieve the trash container and my glasses. Apparently the force of gravity, reacting to the extra weight of my hairdo, caused me to lose my balance, and *whoops!*

I fell in, headfirst. Only my pride got hurt—the old newspapers, cereal boxes, cantaloupe rinds, and rotten tomatoes cushioned my body. Unfortunately, they also cushioned my beehive. The stylist had voided onto my head an entire can of hairspray, which now served as glue holding a fine sprinkling of coffee grounds and mysterious, unidentified decaying matter.

I began to yell for help, but no one came. I sat in there for several hours. Since only single, working people lived in this apartment complex, no one heard me. Eventually, a maintenance man heard me and helped me. I giggled nervously as he pulled me out, self-consciously wondering if I dared introduce myself as "white trash."

Naaah.

I liked living with Al, so I decided to stay in Texas. But about that time, the Lone Star State began to experience a teacher surplus. I had received good job offers from school districts in Minnesota, but I refused to return to my starring role as Nanook of the North.

To get a job in Texas, I knew I had to do something extraordinary. So I got a degree in Generic Special Education, and then I headed to Mexico to teach. I figured learning Spanish couldn't hurt my chances of getting a job when I got back.

While I loved many things about Mexico and its rich culture, I missed the good ole U.S.A. So I headed back to the States, where I managed to land a job working at a school that needed a bilingual teacher with a generic special education degree. Guess what? It was in Texas!

Al and I did our best to keep laughing in the midst of an otherwise painful time. We tried to "make the most" of a tough time. Today when I face difficulties, I realize that being a Christian gives me even more reason to live above my circumstances.

The Apostle Paul faced much more difficult trials as he sat in a Roman prison. Yet he proved that even in the worst times our most important priority must not be our own comfort. He never asked the churches to pray for his speedy release. Instead, he requested, "pray . . . that God may open a door for our message, so that we may proclaim the mystery of Christ, for which I am in chains" (Col. 4:3). Paul wanted more opportunities to do the very activity that landed him in prison!

Instead of asking for our trials to end, we need to focus on using our circumstances to share God's grace with others. As the nineteenth-century clergyman Phillips Brooks once said, "Do not pray for easy lives; pray to be stronger people. Do not pray for tasks equal to your powers; pray for powers equal to your tasks."

Are Teachers Trainable Too?

*D*uring my first year, I taught children considered "trainably mentally retarded" or "TMR." They had IQs between 30 and 50. Being generically handicapped, they had visual and hearing impairments, or any multitude of ailments.

Educators often say, "The best chance a TMR child has is to end up in an institution somewhere. If you can train this child to feed himself and go to the bathroom, you will have a success."

I said, "Baloney. There's a person in there. All people are interested in feeling good about who and what they are." I asked, "Do you want to spend a day putting a nut and bolt together? No. Does someone need to do that? Yes. It's a perfect vocation for that person. They need to touch; they need repetition. At the end of the day they get a check for $5. For them, it's a major accomplishment. They have feelings of self-worth. There is a place for everybody's learning style."

I loved my kids. I had waited my whole life to be a teacher. Now, at age 22, I had my own classroom full. What more could I ask? So I threw myself into my job with a passion. I would arrive at 7 A.M. and leave long after everyone had gone home. Even though, at best, my students faced institutionalization, I took my job teaching them very seriously.

I made a decision early to try to give them more than just survival skills. I obtained permission to cook meals in our room. We built our own furniture. And I tried to help my "children" to become as functional as possible.

I had my moments of questioning this decision, not to mention my sanity. One Monday morning, I'd just finished redecorating my bulletin boards, and I stood back to admire them, thinking they looked pretty nice. Soon my students arrived. Suddenly one of my Down's syndrome children began going into "pretend" labor. She lay there with her dress pulled up, screaming that she was having a baby. She writhed and wailed. While I tried desperately to convince her she wasn't even pregnant, a hyperactive child ran around tearing down all my bulletin boards. Then a child with a glass eye came running up to tell me something, and his eye popped out, hit me in the chest, and rolled around on the floor.

So I began to see that teaching was going to present some interesting challenges. And in the middle of trying to adjust my expectation level about teaching—and life in general—I learned from my doctor that I had physical problems which would probably prevent me from ever giving birth.

I decided to take all that mothering energy and start a home school where severely handicapped children could live with me and be trained in some kind of sheltered employment instead of being institutionalized. I did this in Minnesota, but in Texas I was told, "Start a 'normal' school and get licensed and accredited, then come back and add this program. We recommend that you start with a preschool."

Unfulfilled expectations. How often they lead us to disappointment. While I taught my students how to live on one level, I found myself sitting behind the pupil's desk in life's school on another. I had to begin learning that sometimes, despite hours of careful planning and preparation, we find ourselves thrown into circumstances in which the world swirls crazily around us.

To innoculate ourselves against the devastation of these hurricanes, we need to schedule time for regular walks or sitting quietly, for breathing deeply, and praying silently. In our "life in the fast lane" culture, we must never forget God's words in Psalm 46:10 — "Be still and know that I am God."

We are students for life. So we need to fight desperately to gain those moments when we can sit in a hushed state and breathe to our Teacher, "Speak, Lord. Your servant is listening."

From Camelot to Christ

I could not birth my own children. I could not have a home school for generically handicapped children — so, now what? Forget Plan A. Scrap Plan B. Let's try Plan C. The state said I could open a preschool to begin fulfilling my dream. I began to research preschools, and in the process I discovered Montessori. It seemed like the best route to go for preschoolers, so I began to get the training.

There were things I loved in Montessori and things about which I felt uncomfortable, but on the whole it seemed to be the most effective system around for little ones. My educational approach had always been multi-sensory and this certainly met that criteria.

I began to search for space to lease for my little preschool. A brand new, beautiful church welcomed us with open arms. The facility was "to die for." It sat on a highly visible street in Dallas, nestled among lots of trees. The classrooms had windows, sinks, bathrooms, and wide hallways — a dream come true. (I know, I know. Only a die-hard teacher gets palpitations over sinks and wide hallways.) We built a playground that overlooked the lake, and ducks and swans enhanced the lovely surroundings. I expected Fred Astaire and Ginger Rogers to appear at any moment doing synchronized dance steps.

I wanted someone to pinch me to be sure this was real. The school grew rapidly and soon filled up the entire building. So we added a second building, complete with pillars, a marble fireplace in my office, as well as chandeliers in each room. It looked like the White House, or at least, Tara in *Gone With the Wind*. I squelched the urge to buy a hoop skirt to complete the look.

My personal life was a fairy tale as well. One of the mysteries of life is that when you want something more than life itself, it often eludes you. Then when you let go of the desire and move on, suddenly, your desire comes chasing after you. So it was with me when it came to men. When I thought I would be a "perfect" wife because I love to cook, make a house a home, and nurture, the "right" man didn't see it. Then when I put all my passions into the school and children, suddenly there were men who wanted to date me, but I didn't want to take the time. But in that season of life, one man did get my attention because he wanted to do the school with me. He was older, good at the business aspect of the school which I did not like, and his children were grown, and so we got married. Now I had a husband, a work partner, and a beautiful home. What more could a person ask for in life?

On an external level, my life felt like Camelot. I had the fastest growing school in Dallas, more students than I could handle, a board that read like the "Who's Who," two buildings filled with classrooms upstairs and down, two playgrounds, a library, computer lab, full accreditation, plans to purchase and build on twenty acres, a handsome husband, a gorgeous home . . . so why did I feel so empty?

The church where we leased space invited us to worship with them. I always thought that a church was a church was a church. I had been raised in the church. But I never felt fulfilled by it. In fact, on my confirmation day as I kneeled at the altar to receive my first Communion, the words, "Is this all there is?" ran through my mind. I even requested an appointment with my pastor. I asked, "Is this it? I feel like there is a treasure chest somewhere and all you have given me is a little jewelry box." I ached to know what I was missing. He assured me that since I had memorized my catechism, I had all I needed.

We visited the church. Seemed friendly enough. Sounds OK. Meanwhile, one of my brothers had gotten "saved" and was warning me to stay away from that church. He said it wasn't really a church, but a cult. How could that be? The people were friendly and sang about "peace on earth." I know they talked about God. What was he talking about?

I began to search for "the light." This particular church promised the light would be found in a number of different avenues and I began to pursue them all. Most of these were "ologies." The light appeared to be at each one at the beginning, but always dead-ended in darkness. "What or where IS the light?" I agonized to know.

Someone said it was in meditation so I began to try that. But every time I tried to concentrate on nothingness, the same picture appeared in my mind — that of Jesus Christ. He was always standing on the calm, quiet water (I have always loved water and it feeds my soul) beckoning me to come. The only problem was that I was on the shore and between us lay many jagged rocks. At first this image annoyed me. Then I began to have arguments with Jesus in my mind. "If You want me to come to You, then You walk over those jagged rocks. I don't want to cut my feet." He continued to motion for me to come.

One night at a party, a man asked me where I attended church. So I told him. He responded by quoting what Jesus had said in John 14:6: "I am the way and the truth and the life. *No one* comes to the Father except through Me."

I glibly responded in my most evolved voice, "Come on. Surely God is bigger than that. We are all on our way back to God. Let's not be so narrow-minded." I felt superior for about a half-second. Then I began to cry.

He took me aside, and I blurted out my feelings about this

image I kept seeing about Jesus and the rocks. He gently responded, "Don't you see that Jesus is calling you?" Was He using AT&T, MCI, Sprint or what? I wasn't so sure I wanted to be called.

This man went to his car and returned with a copy of C.S. Lewis' book, *Mere Christianity*. That night I stayed up all night reading it. At dawn, I prayed, "Jesus, *if* You are the *only* way, the truth, and the life, make Yourself real to me." As I entered the church, I felt the enemy for the first time. If you don't know the Lord, you cannot know the enemy. I hit my knees and began to cry. I prayed to accept Christ as my personal Lord and Savior. Then, because I still thought I needed to do good works to gain heaven, I vowed, "Lord, if it takes the rest of my life, I will make this up to You."

I had not yet read the truth in Ephesians 2:8-9, which says, "For it is by grace you have been saved . . . it is the gift of God . . . not by works, so that no one can boast." In other religions, converts obey because they hope to gain something — mainly heaven, or its equivalent. Their prophets have been dead and buried for centuries.

As I grew as a Christian, I discovered that Christ has already paid the price in full for me. And He went on to conquer death and continue to live. I began to see that for the believer, obedience stems from a heart full of gratitude for the gift of grace, rather than from a need to perform in order to be accepted.

Born to Zone

The words "Born to Zone" must be stamped across my forehead in invisible ink. Maybe this is why I am having an identity crisis. In my opinion, there's a good reason why "zone" is a four-letter word.

When I moved our school from the New Age location, I didn't plan to move it into the Dark Ages. But try as I would, I always ran into obstacles. Each potential new location required zoning changes which we had insufficient financial resources to solve. At that time, Dallas' zoning laws were changing in a way that was unfriendly to private schools, as they directly competed with the public school systems.

We finally found a location that was — Praise the Lord — already zoned for a school. After we moved in, however, the city began to fight us because our school went up to higher grades than the previous school. But God intervened and we won.

We outgrew that facility the first year. So we began to look for an even larger facility. Negotiations with place after place got bogged down with zoning laws that required attorneys to interpret. I believe tuition money should go for education and not for political mazes, so I backed away from each of those places. After much prayer, we decided to simply lease space in a large church until the zoning wars ceased.

We ended up at a beautiful place in North Dallas where the largest Christian school in town had previously been located. *No problem. This should be a cinch.* We talked with the "powers that be" at City Hall, and they confirmed that we could move in without any red tape. We decided to move our preschool there and run our elementary and junior high programs in another church, which also had zoning clearance.

We erected a new playground at both locations. And we carpeted and painted the second location. We worked all summer preparing for the opening of two schools. The first day of school at the elementary/junior high location, we received notice that the neighbors were fighting the zoning which allowed for a school to be in the church. I went around all week talking with them to see if we could all win in this situation. But they had already made up their minds. Theirs had been a quiet street with little traffic, and they wanted to keep it that way. So we routed the traffic through the church driveway so parents wouldn't drive through the neighborhood. We were in the middle of resolving this conflict when a new senior pastor came to the church. He did not want the neighbors to oppose the church, so we were informed that we would have to move.

The school year had already started and we moved as many students as we could to the Grace location, and found schools for the other students. This was very traumatic for me since I had to say good-bye to some students that I had had for many years. I found myself waking up in the middle of the night in tears because I was so sad. Gradually the Lord began to show me that having one school, and a small one, was giving me lots more time for my own family which really was my heart's number-one desire. I began to relax and enjoy having one smaller school for the first time in many years until that fateful day. . . .

A neighborhood movement in Dallas gained momentum. If local groups could get enough power, they could change zoning in their areas. The neighborhood at Grace feared we would grow back to our normal size or to the size of the previous school located at Grace. So they began to oppose us. Once again I went door to door. I heard the same story: "We are not opposed to an elementary school, but we don't want a high school." So we restricted ourselves to a tight, legally bound contract that limited our growth to an elementary school only. It seemed so reasonable . . . until I met the leader of the opposition. She put her finger in my face and spit out these words: "You think you are so spiritual. Well let me tell you something. I am the leader of the New Age movement in this town, and we are going to crush you."

That's when I realized this battle had nothing to do with logic. It was clearly a spiritual battle. "For our struggle is not against flesh and blood, but against the rulers, against the authorities, against the powers of this dark world and against the spiritual forces of evil in the heavenly realms," wrote Paul in Ephesians 6:12. So much of the battles of our lives take place in the unseen world.

But we fight a winning battle. God is stronger than the evil forces.

I cried, "Lord, You called me to educate children. That does not tire me. But endless zoning cases and meetings with attorneys waste my time and energy. I can't go through this again." God answered by sending in an army to fight. The Rutherford Institute took our case, saving us nearly $100,000 in attorney's fees. All of the Christian organizations in Dallas, as well as thousands around the country, rallied for our cause. Many devoted their time, energy, and prayers on our behalf. At our hearings, we had the largest turnout in Dallas' history. It made the 10 o'clock news and the front pages of the papers. Tom Landry, Senator Leedom, Dr. Tony Evans, and many others testified for us. In the end, we won.

But I felt weary. I had three young children, and I had

dreams of being a stay-at-home mommy. I wanted out.
Someone gave me a shirt with messages on both sides:

BORN TO ZONE
and
I SURVIVED THE ZONING BATTLE OF '88

I could still laugh, but my fire was gone. This didn't mean
I had allowed myself to be defeated. It meant God was using my exhaustion to guide me into rethinking the current
direction of my life.

To conclude the school story part of this book, let me sum
it up for those of you who like and need closure: I first
wanted the school to be a school for multi-handicapped
children, but the state said to begin as a preschool. This led
me to starting a secular Montessori school located in a
church as well as adjoining property that was owned by a
New Age organization. This led to a detour into the New
Age. The school grew quickly to grade 6 with a waiting list
and plans were underway to build on 20 acres. Then I accepted the Lord Jesus Christ as my personal Savior and de-
sired for the school to be a Christian school. Thus began a
very dark time in which the forces of evil were unleashed
toward the school and me. Many stories could be told from
this time, but God was faithful and delivered us. We moved
to a location that was old and required a great deal of reno-
vation, but on the bright side, it had a pool!

This is where the school began with a Christian founda-
tion based on biblical principles. Even amidst the intense
spiritual warfare, God allowed us to grow spiritually as well
as in grades. We grew to the 9th grade, had a full library,
computer lab, two playgrounds, received accreditation and
had a full curriculum which included Bible. Our curriculum
included all the basics as well as a strong enrichment program which consisted of music, Spanish and P.E., and computers being taught every day. We did lots of musicals, had
a band and choir, and took yearly trips, including one to
Washington, D.C. Our approach with all subjects was to

blend the traditional approach with the multi-sensory and each child's program was individualized. But we had no place to grow. This led us to a three-year search for a new location which eventually resulted in us going into two separate churches with two separate schools. Due to zoning law changes, we ended up with one school at Grace.

I resigned after the "zoning wars" because I felt the Lord calling me into a different kind of ministry. I first served as the Director of Children's Ministry at Grace and then began to write and speak. During the interim the school had two other principals and went through many changes. The Lord brought forth a godly woman with a great deal of experience at other schools and the school is growing back to its former size. I praise the Lord for her leadership.

As I reflect on the history of the school, I see it as an allegory of a person's growth in the Lord as well. We start out thinking we can do it on our own. This time of innocence, combined with pride, may lead us to making many mistakes. Without the guiding light of the Lord to lead and direct us, we may take turns down some precarious paths which can lead to much pain. But God is faithful. He has a purpose and a plan, plans to prosper us and not to harm us (Jer. 29:11). I believe that my time in the school represented a season in which I needed to be called to a death to self. The children consistently brought me much joy and fulfillment, but along with that aspect of the school, there was also much pain, hard work, suffering, and sorrow. But, just as the old hymn says, it is so good to trust in Jesus. He truly is the way, the truth, and the life.

As a society we tend to want to run from pain, but it is through our pain that God grows us and draws us close to Himself. I have learned to embrace the pain knowing that God is the ultimate safety net below. How blessed it is to trust in Jesus. Yes, perhaps I was "born to zone," but each of us is born in the flesh in order to learn to die of the flesh and be born of the spirit. It isn't always a pleasurable process, but one worth investing in. Let's face, it certainly reaps dividends for eternity!

The
Perils
of
Pregnancy

I have always believed that there is nothing more beautiful than a pregnant woman, a new-born baby, or a mother nursing. I spent many an hour in my childhood fantasizing about these miracles. I used to go to sleep at night with a pillow under my baby-doll pajamas, so I could "feel" pregnant. I must confess that even in college I would often rock one of my dolls and listen to music to relax at night. So when my doctor told me I was not put together to conceive easily, if at all, I felt cheated out of the primary reason for my existence. So I took all my intense mothering energy and threw it all into caring for children. Their needs were great and constant, and so was the degree of my mothering energy.

During the intense spiritual warfare time after I became a Christian and wanted to convert the school, my personal life began to unravel as well. In my zeal as a "baby Christian," I wanted it to be a Christian school. My husband did not share my passion and decided it was time we went our separate ways. This was another trial, because as a Christian, I certainly did not want to be divorced. After a time of separation, he decided to file for divorce. We spent our last night together reflecting upon the lovely times. We discussed our mutual decision that he would keep the home and furniture, and I would get the school. Strange as this may seem, our last night was pleasant, and we shared it together as man and wife for the last time. God had a surprise in store for us, however.

My husband did file, and because I did not contest the divorce, it was finalized in only two months. Before long, I began to feel sleepy, then nauseous. At first I thought I had a little bug. But after four weeks, I figured it was more than just a little bug. I thought it must be an emotional response to the divorce. But after four months, I convinced myself that I had cancer or some other dread disease. So I went to the doctor. After running every other test known to mankind, he ran a pregnancy test as a last resort. Apparently, that last night together as husband and wife had brought the beginning of a new little life.

When I first found out I was pregnant, I felt stunned. This was the greatest miracle of my life. I had gone to see the doctor thinking I was dying of cancer, and I left knowing I had a life growing inside of me. This was the most awesome feeling ever. Never mind that I was no longer married. Yes, the child had been conceived in marriage, but I was definitely divorced now. Even that realization could not negate the high I felt.

I called my former husband from the doctor's office to find out what we should do. I believed God had intervened because He didn't want us to be divorced. As a baby Christian, and now a baby soon-to-be Christian school principal, divorce certainly could not be part of God's perfect plan for my life. I was sure of it.

My former husband was not so convinced. In all fairness, I do not in any way want to represent him as a "bad guy." He is a wonderful man. We were simply at cross-seasons of life. Part of his attraction to me was my inability to conceive. He was older, his children had grown, and he had grandchildren. My being pregnant at a season of life when he was ready to retire was "not in the cards." He did not share my passion for having a Christian school, and he felt he was long past the season for fatherhood. He had divorced me and wanted it kept that way, but promised to help with the child. I realized that he really wasn't ready for this child that I wanted more than life itself. I had seen children torn apart by divorce and going back and forth between two homes. I did not want that for my child. In the same friendly manner in which we had parted, we decided that I would raise this child on my own. I have always been deeply appreciative of his willingness to let me have it this way. Of course, I wanted a father for my child, but I felt strongly that this child should not have to shuffle back and forth between two homes and two different lifestyles. If my ex-husband wanted us to remain divorced, then I wanted the "say-so" in the raising of our child.

But soon the reality of my aloneness began to hit home. Being by myself has never bothered me; in fact, I crave solitude. But this should have been the happiest season of my life, and I wanted to share it with someone. My best friend ministered to me, but she didn't know the Lord at the time, and while I appreciated her help and love in every way, I longed to commune on the level of sisters in Christ.

She and I went out to celebrate, since I was out of my mind with elation over being pregnant. As we enjoyed our ice cream cones, I vowed, "This is the very last bit of junk food that will ever pass these lips. I am going to have a healthy pregnancy, nurse this child, and be the best, wisest mother in the universe." The next night over another ice cream cone, I said the same thing, and the next. . . .

As my pregnancy progressed, I discovered that the only foods I could keep down were French fries and Coke — and of course my nightly ice cream cone, which I needed for the protein and calcium, naturally. But I swore to myself, "As soon as I quit being the leading contender for the Guinness record in 'Frequency of Upchucking,' boy, will I ever eat healthy."

Our school housed the Lamaze classes for the citywide organization. So I devoured every one of their books and viewed the films a few thousand times. This Mother Earth was getting ready. I decided that continuing to live in my office and sleep on the floor might have to come to an end. I had to have a home for this child. At night I had long talks with the Lord and this unborn child. Together, we were going to get through this.

I had been worried about the possibility that no Christians would enroll in my soon-to-be Christian school because of our prior New Age associations and my spiritual past. Now, these loomed smaller in comparison to the obstacles of being the D-word (divorced) and now the P-word (pregnant!). I was going to be the laughingstock of this city. Who in their right minds would send their kids to this school?

I continued to throw up night and day. I continued to feel alone. But during that time, I began to learn to keep my focus on only the Lord Jesus Christ. It was the beginning of a lifelong journey of His teaching me that it doesn't matter what people say and think, it only matters that I stay close to Him and walk with Him. I devoured the Word like a dehydrated person on the desert finding a pool of cool, clear water.

Pregnancy wasn't turning out like I thought it would. In fact, it was a drag. When I first realized I was pregnant, I thought I had invented it. I thought I had singlehandedly pulled off the coup of a lifetime. I soon realized what God had done, and I stood in awe of Him as the ultimate Creator. I did have a few questions about His divine timing, however. . . .

After the state of elation passed and I got beyond the state of "awe," I began to discover the perils of pregnancy. Yes, it was great to let my tummy hang out because it was *supposed* to. That felt real good. And who cared if my pants were tight—I'd just let out the elastic string. But what about the constant state of nausea? That got old. What about the leg cramps that awakened me in the middle of the night? At least they distracted me from the backaches. There I was, the thinnest time of my adult life, and no one appreciated it.

(I often wonder why the most effective diet for me was pregnancy.) The last thing on my mind was dating or even having a male look at me.

I did begin to sense a new appreciation for the state of womanhood. I began to look at other women in a new light. My mother had gone through this multiple times, and I had a new found new respect for her. Instead of envying her, I now lifted my hands in applause. I wondered — how could a woman care for another baby while also pregnant? To me, *she* became the ultimate Wonder Woman.

There's something very comforting in the knowledge that others have gone before us, faced the same or greater difficulties, and survived to encourage us that we can make it. I think it's this same feeling the Apostle Paul acknowledged when he wrote, "Praise be to the God and Father of our Lord Jesus Christ, the Father of compassion and the God of all comfort, who comforts us in all our trouble, so that we can comfort those in any trouble with the comfort we ourselves have received from God" (2 Cor. 1:3-4).

Enter
Stage
Right...
Paul

*I*t was now the Fourth of July in the hottest year of recorded history in Texas. Another day of 107 degree weather, with a heat index of 100,000 times mc². I tried to get off my bed long enough to take a friend's children to see fireworks. During the show, I told God that I felt really sick and tired of being sick and tired. If He could just send some energy my way, I could get this school ready to be a Christian school. As it was, the thought of that mountain to climb, along with all the others, seemed overwhelming. But God, as He so often does, gave me peace that night that He was with me and that somehow everything would turn out OK.

The next morning I woke up feeling like my good "old self," ready to take on the world. A smile came back to my face and a bounce to my walk. *Yes, with the Lord, I can face life again.*

That week a friend asked me to dinner. She felt sorry for me because I had no Christian friends, and even though she was not a believer, she knew a man named Paul who was. She arranged for all of us to have dinner. *OK, so maybe I can have my French fries and Coke with someone instead of all alone.*

So we met. After the introduction, I instructed this stranger in my usual discreet and sophisticated way that if I rushed from the table quickly, not to take offense.

The night was pleasant. Paul and I stood in the parking lot long after my friend went home. We talked about the Lord for hours. He had been raised in a Christian home. His father had been on staff at Dallas Theological Seminary ("Oh really, what is that?") for 27 years. His dad rode to work with Howie Hendricks, and Chuck Swindoll mowed the grass. ("Really? You're kidding! Wow!")

I shared with him my dream to open a Christian school, but also told him that I seemed totally ineffective in converting others. He listened. He counseled. We became good friends. He took me to his church. That first Sunday, the pastor came over to meet me. Paul's parents stood trying to figure out how to introduce me, as by now I was definitely "great with child."

"This is Paul's . . . ah . . er . . . ah . . friend."

We got lots of interesting looks. And I am sure we provided some fascinating dinner conversation for various members of the congregation. (Ten years later, this same church asked me to be their Director of Children's Ministries. I wonder if God chuckled as He watched those awkward introductions that first Sunday.)

It was a special time for Paul's parents. They had a son on the mission field with Sudan Interior Mission in Africa, and that daughter-in-law's due date was near mine. So, they shared in her pregnancy vicariously through me. They were most gracious and understanding about their son hanging out with an unmarried, pregnant woman. They eased the tension by cracking jokes such as, "Well, at least we don't have to worry about you getting this girl pregnant!"

My parents, of course, wanted to know this nice man who was being so kind to their poor, pregnant daughter. So we met them on Thanksgiving, and that went beautifully.

We knew I needed to get a place where I could have separate bedrooms for the baby and me. So Paul helped me find and move into a little place. On that Sunday, we still had more things to move, so we decided to skip church "just this once." I went down to school to rummage up some boxes. When I entered, things seemed kind of strange. I kept hearing sounds from behind the building, so I called the police. Someone was robbing us. It became quite a scene. Our school sat across the street from a huge church. As that church concluded their services, police cars arrived, robbers attacked police, and people saw blood. There I stood in my rotund state with robbers screaming at me, "You'll pay for this."

And I did. The threatening calls came night and day. At first I didn't take them seriously, but then they scared me. I had police surveillance. Paul became worried about me and checked on me frequently. We had to go to court. It was another trial. I felt constantly afraid. My only distraction was that it was time to begin the Lamaze classes. Paul knew I had signed up to take them, so he asked if I wanted his help. I thought that was so sweet and caring. So we took the classes together. (Another aside: After we became friends with the instructor and her husband, we learned that she had felt angry, thinking Paul had fathered my child but had refused to marry me!)

I began to look forward to Christmas and imagined holding my little one, who was due on Christmas Day. One week before the *big day*, I got very sick. Paul brought me some soup and took care of me. Finally, after three days, I could sit up. That afternoon, I sat in a chair wearing no makeup, looking really ragged. He came over and got on his knees and proposed! Of course, I thought he was kidding. But he wasn't. It had never occurred to me that anyone would want me in this pitiful condition, especially now. I had made peace with the fact that I was having this child alone and was not looking to be "rescued."

Better pray about this.

God gave both of us peace about this next chapter. Our parents were supportive. And it all seemed like a fairy tale.

Even though I felt ugly and unlovable, Paul thought I was beautiful.

Paul was not unlike God in His love and compassion. When His children were at their worst, God spoke through Ezekiel reminding Israel that she was His bride, saying, "I gave you beautiful clothes of linens and silk . . . I gave you lovely ornaments, bracelets, and beautiful necklaces . . . and a lovely tiara for your head. . . . You became very beautiful and rose to be a queen" (Ezek. 16:10-14, TLB).

God loves us for better and for worse. He cares about us in sickness and in health. He cherishes us both in times of abundance and emptiness. Like a devoted groom, God has made a commitment to us that will never fail.

Here Comes the Bride, Big, Fat, and...

*W*ith the first marriage, I had a fairy tale wedding. But I didn't know the Lord Jesus Christ in a personal way. This time I *knew* the Lord was blessing this union, and I had peace. Strange a time as it was, I wanted very much to marry Paul. We never had a chance to date and do the normal things couples do during a courtship, but my life didn't seem to be following the normal course of events in any other way, so why should this be any different? We decided to "do" this wedding with a Justice of the Peace and then have a "real" ceremony with Paul's father officiating when I wasn't so big, fat, and wide.

Now, what to wear? A friend had lent me a cranberry red dress to wear for Christmas in case my little one decided to be late. Paul had not seen that dress.

"Yes," I thought, "that would be something special. Most brides do not get married in a red dress, but after all it is Christmas and after all . . . *most* brides are not three centimeters dilated!"

Paul, likewise, had decided to wear something "special." For him, this translated into a green suit that I had never seen. When he picked me up, we doubled over laughing. As if we needed to draw any more attention to ourselves.

It was a cold, windy day and I couldn't get my coat around me, which added to the hilarity of the situation. Decked out with my *huge,* beautiful orchid that Paul put on my *huge* red dress, and with Paul in his green suit we set out for downtown Dallas. It seemed like a good day to get married. The marriage license line was long, and I felt tempted to feign labor pains to get to the front of the line. But after one look at us, everyone moved us to the head of the line anyway.

Even in the strangeness of this wedding, I still dreamed of a bit of beauty and magic. God decided we needed to be married in the office of a Justice of the Peace who had razor-back pigs adorning his walls. This was too much. The JP took one look at us, and while trying to keep his eyes from drifting to my tummy, he read the vows at an alarming speed. In the same breath as "I now pronounce you man and wife," he finished the sentence with, "That will be $10 please." I think he feared that my water would break right there in his office. I am sure he thought we were pagans who simply were out of God's will and he probably prayed for our salvation as well as a safe delivery. We got out of there and laughed until we collapsed in the hallway.

Then we went out for brunch, assuming that by evening this little one would decide to be born. The teachers held a special dinner for us that night, and everyone seemed happy. Obviously we could not consummate the marriage, so we sat drinking grape juice and ate homemade bread as our special "last meal." It had been a fun day—but no baby.

The next day we moved Paul into my place. The day after that my parents arrived. Then Christmas came. Still no baby. I began to have nightmares that this child would never come out. I drank cod liver oil. I took long walks. I ate large meals. Each was "sure" to make the baby come. Finally my doctor said, "Go ahead and consummate the marriage. Maybe the baby will decide to come." Now *there's* a romantic thought. Making love with a woman who looks like a beached whale — isn't that every man's dream?

Eventually I became convinced that this child wanted to be the first baby born in 1981, so we could get all the special gifts. NOT. The first day back at school after the holidays found me, once again, standing outside supervising morning car lines. In response to each brilliant parent who gasped and said, "You mean you haven't had that baby yet?" I glibly replied, "Oh, yeah, I had mine, but it was so much fun being pregnant, I opened a service and I now carry other women's babies." After two weeks, no one laughed — especially not me. I figured this child was blind and could not find the "exit" sign.

Paul and I had decided to have a LeBoyer birth. Only two doctors in Dallas did those, and we selected the one closest to where we lived. He was going to do a photo essay book on LeBoyer births and asked if I would like to be in this book. "Of course," I said. (Remember, I was born with a camera cord around my neck instead of an umbilical cord.) I still had the illusion that I was Mother Earth.

Waiting. Waiting. More waiting. It seems that Christians spend most of their lives waiting. In fact, the Psalms are filled with exhortations to "wait on the Lord" or "wait patiently for the Lord." God's timing usually isn't anything like what we imagine or expect it will be. But Solomon reminds us in Ecclesiastes, "He has made everything beautiful in its time" (3:11). And I had one great hope besides the Lord — no one stays pregnant forever.

Mother Earth Gives Birth

*Y*ou want me in your photo essay book, doc? Sure! Just let me touch up my makeup before the shots, OK?"

I was ready. *Breathe, one, two, three. I've got this down.* I had my bag packed (for six weeks now!) with music, candles, and a pretty gown. Eventually I had to take out the Christmas decorations, since we were well into January. I had to let go of my fantasy of nursing this child by the Christmas tree. There we were, newlyweds, and my parents were *still* staying with us awaiting this wondrous birth. But no baby. Finally this little one began to head toward the exit sign. We were ready. Whoops! The baby wasn't. Just a warmup, but not the *real thing.* Time to go back home. What a drag. I was definitely *not* having fun. I went to sleep and guess what—finally the real thing!

"Hey, wait a minute! This hurts." It's hard to apply mascara while doubling over. "OK, breathe, one, two, three." I am a "toucher" so I had told Paul, "Just touch me and I will be fine. This will be *no big deal.* I was born for this."

I had read every book on the subject. I began to feel a little upset that authors had deleted a few rather important details such as, "You might get the shakes and convulsions." That is especially hard to capture on film.

After my third day in labor, I was definitely getting weary of the whole deal. The mascara was long gone, my hair was matted against my head, and I couldn't have cared less about the stupid photo essay book.

I retreated deep into myself. Paul just sat and stared, wondering where I had gone. The only words I could say were, "I really love you, but don't touch me." My only conscious thought was, "I am dying. I need to get this child out of me so I can die. Yes, that is a good plan." It seemed like the only logical thought within me.

In all fairness to my doctor, I had given him strict instructions: "I want this baby a la naturale. Do NOT give me any medication, no matter how much I beg for it." Of course, that was when I thought the baby would come on time and we were going to be home for Christmas. Unbeknownst to me, another doctor who had his children in my school was pacing outside my room screaming at my doctor, "Get that baby out or you will lose both of them." They came in.

"Jody, 'come to' for a minute; we want you to participate in this decision or Paul will have to make it for you. We have to get this baby out now. You still have two choices: an epidural and forceps *or* a C- section." I didn't like my choices but I didn't exactly like the process either. I moaned "the first."

Paul said he watched a transformation before his very eyes. I had not opened my eyes once all day or night. As the epidural took effect, I opened my eyes, looked around, asked for a mirror, began making jokes, put on makeup, and asked where the cameras had gone for the book. (They, of course had abandoned the idea, realizing this was no Mother Earth they were dealing with.) Now I was ready. What was the holdup? My doctor friend in the hall was sure the baby had died since other women who'd had the same flu I had in December had given birth to stillborns. I am glad I didn't know that. My holdup was the same physical reason my original doctor thought I could not conceive. I had a piece of tissue blocking the birth canal.

"We know the whole creation has been groaning as in the pains of childbirth right up to the present time," wrote Paul in Romans 8:22. Giving birth without medication is more overrated than honeymoons. In fact, it's about the most physically painful experience a woman will ever have. I think that's why the apostle uses the analogy of childbirth when he tells us that the whole creation writhes in this same kind of intense, unspeakable pain with groanings — which would be screams, if screams didn't use so much energy. But that's not the end of the story. Just as rejoicing over a new life usually makes us quickly forget the pain of birth, we have a great hope that "our present sufferings are not worth comparing with the glory that will be revealed in us" (Rom. 8:18). One day all believers and all creation will rejoice over our new, completely redeemed status, and we can cease forever from our groaning the groans of pain over this life in its fallen state.

ICU
and
Other
Traumas

*O*nce the forceps moved the blockage, my son slipped out in a second. In fact, the doctor barely had time to catch him, he came so fast. Him? Did I say *him*? I had been talking to a *girl* for these past months. I had been calling her Emily Lynelle. A boy? A long, skinny boy? I smiled. He looked just like my daddy. God had given me a reflection of my father, whom I loved so much.

That night as I held Christopher, my friend, Kay, "sneaked in" and gave me two gifts. As I looked at them, I felt God's hand of blessing as they seemed to foreshadow His plan for Christopher David — a pair of basketball sneaker booties and a shirt that said, "God's Little Messenger." Today Christopher is an excellent basketball player who truly is God's *big* messenger. The night was magic as I held him and pondered the mystery of God. Yes, His timing had seemed strange, but I could see how He had taken a seemingly bleak situation and turned it into a miraculous blessing. My cup truly ran over, and I didn't seemed to notice the exhaustion — until the doctors came in to check Christopher.

"Mrs. Capehart, because Christopher was so long over-due, the uterus failed to adequately nourish him. Something is wrong. We need to take him to ICU."

Suddenly I felt pain *everywhere*.

"We planned a LeBoyer birth to have a quiet entry into this crazy, mixed-up world. Now you are taking my child from me to hook him up to machines and bright lights and beepers for twenty-four hours a day? You *have* to be kidding!"

Another question for God: Why was I the *only* woman on the floor who could *not* have her baby with her, yet I had been placed in a room with a woman who invited her entire country of origin to share in the joy of her *twin* girls. Every time one of them cried (and they had perfectly synchronized schedules so each carefully put in twelve hours), my milk would get going. This is the other thing they forget to tell in the books—how I would feel *after* the birth. Oh, yes, they all talk about the postpartum blues. But what about the double episiotomy from the forceps that kept me from being able to "function" on my own. Or, when my milk came in response to the twins' cries, and I ended up producing enough to feed all of Ethiopia. I felt convinced that before long they would need to get me a larger room just to house my ever-growing breasts.

Well, I wasn't going to take it anymore. At 3 A.M. when the twins screamed *once again,* and my bra size had increased to 60 XYZ, and I was *once again* trying to tinkle but couldn't, I decided to move swiftly into action. I marched right down to the nurses' station and demanded to know, "Why am I the *only* woman on the floor who can*not* have her baby with her, and why am I sharing a room with a woman who has *two?*" (God in His sense of humor later had these same nurses serve on a board with me—they love to retell this story.)

The next morning, they told Paul to get me into a private room and then take me to the shower to reduce my breast size. It's an interesting phenomenon—actually *being* a milkshake. But I felt better. My attitude improved. That night we had a lovely dinner (OK, he brought in food from the "outside" world) and wondered when we would ever be able to take our son home. It broke our hearts to see him hooked up to all those machines. We longed to hold him and take him out of there.

My parents were wonderful. They had come for a December birth and to celebrate Christmas. Then they had patiently waited for a month and still they could not hold their precious grandson. The waiting felt long for everyone.

· That night I tiptoed down to the ICU to talk to Christopher. I told the night nurse that if I could just hold him and nurse him, I felt he could begin to get better. She agreed. She took him off the machines and brought him to me. I held and nursed him all night. At 5 A.M., he went back to ICU. Two hours later, when they checked him, he showed signs of improvement. "What a miracle of medical science," they said. *Well, think what you want, dear doctors, I know what made my son start to heal.*

More tests.

"There is a pretty good chance of brain damage, Mrs. Capehart."

Today as I look at my thirteen-year-old son, a straight-A student, a fine athlete, and very tall for his age, I haven't seen the signs yet. But that day looking at him in ICU, I faced the harsh reality that he probably would have some damage. But I knew I would love him all the same. *Is this why God trained me in special education?* It didn't matter. I just praised the Lord for the gift of life and a son whom I couldn't love any more than I did.

Finally, they took him out of intensive care, and we went home.

Why did God allow my son to get better, while many around me that week did not have the happy endings for which they had hoped and prayed? I promise you it was not because my faith was any greater than theirs. You might say God allowed them to suffer so they could grow, come to know Him, or have opportunities to glorify Him.

And that's all true. But when pain is intense, why doesn't that seem to be enough?

I think it helps to recognize that part of suffering is a mystery. In Isaiah 55:9, God says, "As the heavens are higher than the earth, so are My ways higher than your ways and My thoughts than your thoughts."

So just how far are the heavens above the earth?

Some scientists estimate that it would take a million years traveling at the speed of light to go from one galaxy to the next. That means it would take us 100 billion trips at the speed of light for 1 million years each to explore the universe.

That's pretty amazing.

We'll never fully figure out why, but it's enough that we know who.

Caring for Christopher

Caring for Christopher has been a joy from day one. He smiles easily, loves everyone, has a great sense of humor, and understands people. He is an excellent athlete, which amazes me since I am not. (In fact, in school I was the LAST one to be picked for the team. Did I say, "picked"? Rather it was, "You HAVE to take Jody." Does a lot for the self-esteem.) In my book, *Cherishing and Challenging Your Children,* I said that Christopher always made me look good as a parent. In reality, he looked good, not me.

We have always shared a very special bond. We can talk for hours and love to take on "deep" subjects. We have the same sense of humor, and both are gregarious around people, but then have strong needs for solitude. We understand each other, and the simpatico of our spirits has truly blessed me. As we have transitioned into the teen years, we are aware that things are changing. But all it takes is for us to have a "date" or for me to take him along on a speaking trip, and our relationship is all back, just as solid as ever. I truly enjoy him as a person and as my son.

Christopher is very funny and and keeps me in stitches.

He cracked me up even before he knew what a joke was or that he was even funny. One of his greatest lines as a child was when I was pregnant with Angela. I had just had a sonogram, which my doctor required at my age. The boys had been playing with their Gobots and Transformers in the corner. Paul and I were looking carefully at the screen to see if it was a girl. Yes, we were happy that she was healthy, but was it a girl??? At 5 P.M., they told me we had to leave, and we still did not have that information. As I was getting down from the table, the monitor picked up a clear shot of her little bottom. There was no doubt that this was a girl. The nurse said, "Freeze that frame. That is the clearest shot of a vagina we have ever seen."

My husband lamented as they took lots of still shots of our daughter, "These photos will dash her hopes of ever being Miss America. . . ." Seriously, we were delighted beyond words, especially after having two boys. We went out to eat and celebrate.

As the waitress came to bring us a menu, Christopher said in this great three-year-old voice, "I am gonna have a sister, and I know it cuz I just saw her 'lasagna.' " I nearly went into labor because I was laughing so hard. Obviously, this was a child's innocent remark and not a joke, but today Christopher still keeps me going with his wit and voice imitations.

Christopher is much like my father, whom I adore. My father tells jokes for hours. One year we timed it to see how long he could go before he repeated a joke. After twelve hours, we fell asleep, and he kept telling jokes and laughing at each one. When he starts a joke, he says, "Have you heard the one about . . . don't tell me if you have because I want to hear it again!" and he laughs warmly. I love to hear him tell jokes. He has just been asked to write a book called "Chet's Chuckles." I'm sure it will be a real blessing, especially to my father, who is having the time of his life writing it. I imagine he will read it each day just to hear the jokes again. I envision him sitting in his chair laughing uproariously.

When the reality of who Christopher's REAL father was dawning upon him, we talked most of the night. That morning he hugged me and said, "I love you, Mom. I am glad I didn't have to go back and forth between two homes. Thank you for sparing me that pain. Mom, who am I most like? I think, Grandpa Kvanli." Yes, my darling. You are a clone of your Grandpa. How abundantly God has blessed me.

However, I do marvel at the sovereignty of God. Even though Paul is not Christopher's biological father, they are a great deal alike. They share a common passion for sports and they especially love to go out golfing and both are excellent golfers, I might add. Christopher is now playing French horn, just like his "daddy." Paul plays French horn in the Dallas Symphony Orchestra. As time has gone on, especially since Christopher got so tall, people say, "Boy he sure is getting to look like his dad." I just smile. Only a loving God could have orchestrated this relationship so perfectly. Paul truly IS Christopher's father.

The Many Dimensions of Damon

Who are the parents of this child?
. . . who lets the other soccer team score while checking out the local flora?
. . . who asks the lady at the grocery store "Why are you so fat?"

. . . who bumps into people at the mall or church or school or anywhere because he walks backward on his toes.

. . . who is sometimes labeled charismatic because he is always speaking in one of his newly developed "Damonized" versions of Ig-pay Atin-lay.

. . . who shows off his manners by picking his food into the tiniest pieces possible with his fingers before eating it. (It goes better with his special drink made up of milk, juice, salt, pepper, Sweet and Low, ketchup, and anything else within reach.)

When I first met Damon, he was six years old. He was Paul's son by a previous marriage. Since children are my passion, connecting with them is usually easy. Not so with Damon. We had our first encounter at the swimming pool. I met Paul and Damon there, assuming we would play and swim. But Damon found another use for the pool, a place to have his father call out fractions so he could give the decimal equivalents. Or when it got really hot, he would have Paul tell him a number so he could provide the square root. Call me strange, but that is not what I usually do at the pool.

It didn't take a degree in chemical engineering to figure out I had met a little genius. But he had no clue about how to be a child. He couldn't play, except with his father, and they played "head games." I loved watching Paul with Damon; he could "connect" with him. Paul tried to introduce music and sports to Damon, but to no avail. I felt proud of Paul for abandoning his expectations for sharing these most important parts of his life with Damon. His only means of connecting with his son was through playing the never-ending academic games. As a person trained in child development, I wanted to hold Damon and get him to play and come out of himself. I failed miserably.

He showed his first sign of needing physical affection once when I was nursing Christopher. He asked me to rock him and nurse him as my baby. He was seven. Call me strange again, but that seemed a little odd to me. We compromised. After I put Christopher in his bed, I would rock Damon and give him a bottle of juice. After a few weeks of this, he said he was done being a baby. (Thank You, Lord!)

Life with Damon always left me a little on the edge. He loved obtuse, abstract subjects but seemed to have little understanding of how to relate to others. He did strange things. For example, our family would go swimming at the school pool on Saturdays. I would put Christopher on a baby raft and swim laps pushing him ahead of me. Once when I needed to use the rest room, I put the raft far away from the pool and asked Damon to watch Christopher for a few moments. As I sat in the stall, I heard a splash and came running. Damon had thrown Christopher in the pool.

"Why?" I asked. (OK, I screamed.)

Damon, always the logical one, simply replied, "To see if he would float."   Cough . . . sputter. . . .

After that, I never left Damon unattended with Christopher. When my mother kept Damon for the first time, he found some matches and decided to find out how many combustible items she possessed. Surely she was happy to participate in such an important research project. My mother is great with kids but, because I dearly love her, and I wanted to keep her around for a few more years, I didn't leave him with her for a while.

Damon was easily distracted, impulsive, and generally lacking in social skills. He believed that all kids hated him, and he did nothing to change that. He always felt like an outcast around other children. He could not relate, and he didn't play.

It took Damon's siblings to heal the child in him and help him learn to be young. Christopher adored Damon. Damon had *zippo* people skills; conversely, Christopher possessed natural people abilities. As Damon learned to play WITH Christopher, he learned to play. Christopher modeled to Damon HOW to play. It took years. Damon really began peaking in this area at about age twelve. In fact, at age eleven, he put toys on his Christmas list for the first time. Why? He wanted to play with them WITH Christopher. Amazing.

Angela thinks he is the greatest person ever. She loves to hug and kiss him. It touches me to see Damon hold her and express affection to her.

Every one of Damon's teachers agreed that he was exceptionally bright but hard to reach. No one could get him to do his work, yet he always knew the answers. What's a teacher to do? I have always believed that children learn best through multi-sensory instruction. Damon did well with the equipment but could not transfer anything to paper. I tried every "teacher" trick I knew to get him to do better in school.

I did not know about A.D.D. at that time. But I discovered that Damon, as a right-brained, auditory, kinesthetic learner, works best with sound, with little light and in an informal work space. This violates what most left-brain teachers think their students need, including me. Damon taught me much about how children learn, especially when traditional methods fail.

I made many mistakes with Damon and have regretted that he didn't enter my life later, when I knew more about A.D.D. He had every symptom. But for someone unfamiliar with A.D.D., it is easy to find these children VERY frustrating, annoying, and "a pain" to have around. You wonder if they hold nightly summit meetings plotting how to most effectively drive you nuts. They are remarkably successful at this.

The child unnerved me at home and at school. I have always been a patient person with children, but I found Damon bringing me to the edge all too frequently. I resented him for bringing out a monster in me I didn't know was there.

As I learned, I became more accepting. I made every mistake possible in the process of trying to learn. But pain is a great teacher.

With adolescence looming, I thought I might as well send myself off to the funny farm. But two dramatic changes occurred. God intervened, and Damon began improving. He began to give affection, talk about his feelings, make eye contact, develop a sense of humor, and make better grades. Why?

1. God poured out His grace.
2. Damon became a Christian at age eleven.
3. He began to feel part of a structured family life.
4. I learned more about A.D.D. and began to deal with him more effectively.
5 He experienced his siblings' love.
6. Church molded him.
7. He discovered his gifts in music and become even more bonded to his father.

Damon received an invitation from Duke University each summer to attend classes for gifted children and he also joined the orchestra and band. He involved himself in church, found a few friends, and began to get good grades. He was invited to be on the academic decathlon team; academically he could handle it, but socially, his behavior still left room for improvement.

Today he is at a university on full scholarship, holds a job, makes good grades, teaches Sunday School and is, frankly, a person I truly love AND like to be around. I find him handsome and charming, and I feel grateful that he is an important part of my life. I am dedicating one of my books on A.D.D. to him, because he taught me so much and made me more effective when I counsel other parents and teachers. I know the pain and frustration. I have been there. And there is hope. People with A.D.D. are some of the most interesting, gifted, and creative people I know. Damon taught me that also.

God created each of us UNIQUE for HIS purpose. People with A.D.D. get the message that they are broken and must be fixed, or that we need to medicate them so WE can live happily ever after. Not so. They are highly gifted people. We just simply have to move out of our traditional left-brained way of trying to label and categorize every person to meet our criteria and pray for God to give us a window to see each person as He created them to be. A.D.D. adds another dimension to the learning puzzle, but it's an exciting one. I feel compelled to help teachers find doors to bring these students through this educational maze we call "school."

God gets us through this maze we call "life on earth" by giving us His grace, opening windows, and closing doors until we begin to find His will for our lives. Let's have the same zeal to reach others for His kingdom, especially those who do not fall within the tight constraints of our comfort zone.

I once told Damon during his teenage years that adolescence may be his most difficult season of life. I said, "You are probably one of those people for whom adolescence will be painful and lonely, but you will really hit your stride once you reach your twenties." Damon is one of those late bloomers whom his peers were not ready to appreciate until he grew some. It gave us both hope to know that the hardest part of his life would be over soon and, praise God, that's just what happened.

It's hard to be a misfit. It's hard to be different from everybody around you. But there is a godly kind of misfit that brings honor to God. In the "Hall of Faith" in Hebrews 11, the writer cites all kinds of misfits who lived for the glory of God, then pronounces on them a touching eulogy: "The world was not worthy of them" (v. 38). Damon reminds me of the importance of esteeming and valuing those who don't fit into the world's mold, because often the very people of whom the world is not worthy are those who will feel right at home in heavenly mansions.

Our Christmas Angel

I love Christmastime best. I've always believed God ordained that Thanksgiving would fall on Thursday so we would have a four-day weekend during which to set up our tree and the other forty-seven boxes of Christmas decorations. During my single years, after I finished decorating my apartment or house, I would put on Barbra Streisand's Christmas album, which closes with "The Best Gift." As that song played, I would rock a doll by the light of the Christmas tree and long for the day when I could hold my own baby under the twinkling lights.

It came as no surprise when my doctor told me Christopher's due date — Christmas Day. My dream had come true. I did feel surprised, however, when he chose to delay his entrance until January 13. On January 8, Paul told me I had to take down the tree since it had only seven needles left on it. I mourned. But since then, I have come to appreciate Christopher's January birthday, because it gives me something to anticipate after the post-Christmas depression sets in.

Angela had a December 7 due date; she came December 13. I finally had my Christmas baby to rock and nurse by the tree. Believe me, I did. I cherished every moment of that sweet time. It was as close to heaven on earth as any experience could be. Angela did not, however, come into the world peacefully. She came out angry, even though we had a completely natural and beautiful birth experience which I will always cherish. As a matter of fact, at the moment of her birth, three tornadoes touched down in Dallas, Texas. One of those was mine. It was an awesome day, weather-wise, and she reflected it. She arrived "loaded for bear." I took one look at her, lay back down, and aged ten years. But after her first bath, as we nursed quietly, I saw my angel. My Christmas angel had arrived; so we named her Angela Elizabeth.

It's probably my fault that she experienced a difficult infancy. In my usual zeal, I took her to school (I was still principal) three days after her birth. And I took her with me at five days old as I taught Sunday School. One week later, she came down with an ear infection and bronchitis. From that time on, she screamed for hours. This continued for months. It becomes difficult to keep an infant in your office when she screams constantly. The junior high kids kept me sane that semester because when they finished their work, they "got to" take Angela for a walk—the only thing that made her happy.

At three months, she "leap-frogged" around the school on her back, using her head as the pivotal point. That worked well for her, since it was so hard. A determined little girl, she rarely smiled. She would often tell adults "No, No," which I think she perceived to be life's key message. She climbed everything, walked at eight months, drank from the dog's dish, and loved it when the German shepherd knocked her over full speed. I wondered what I had birthed, and the image of my Christmas angel faded.

I could never describe life with Angela as dull. She was a disaster seeking a place to hit. Once when I stopped to get gas, she wiggled out of her car seat and fell out of the car. It hurt the pavement, but didn't do much sustaining damage to her.

One night after six hours of nonstop screaming (yes, the sound came from vocal cords of both mother and child), I decided to try a home remedy someone had recommended. I diluted it, but when I gave it to her, she went catatonic and quit breathing. I nearly did also, and in my last breath, screamed for my husband. The emergency room staff told us to keep getting water down her. After a minute, she began to breathe again. Then, for the next few hours, she provided us with a symphony of remarkable "tooting" and burping. Amazingly, as she exhaled, bubbles came out . . . big bubbles. I still felt so shell-shocked, I didn't even rush to grab my camera. (This is the only Kodak moment I have missed in my entire life.) It surely would have won a photo contest.

Once when I went to pick up Christopher from a birthday party at an indoor amusement park, she darted away from me. I frantically hunted for her in a jungle of people. Finally, I heard "Mama!" and there she stood, at the TOP of a ride that went up and down. She stood up there, balanced perfectly at ten months, much to the shock of everyone— especially me. I bought Velcro and attached her to me for the next year. Where, oh where, did my Christmas angel go?

With her chronic ear infections and incredible energy and tenacity, I felt convinced she had acquired an allergy to sleep. She never slept for more than two hours at a stretch her first year. My husband and I became so weary that our memories of that year are a blur. The only thing I could say to cheer myself was, "At least I didn't have twins."

Finally, I relented and we decided to have tubes put in her ears. Christopher always came to our room during the night, even at age one. Angela never did. She just screamed. I tried lying down with her in the guest bedroom, but she would have nothing to do with it. Yet the night before her surgery, she came to our bed. She just sat there and stared at us. She didn't talk. She knew something was up and wasn't sure how she felt about it. Nothing would comfort her. But at least she didn't scream.

The doctor said she came out of anesthesia faster than any child he had ever seen. While still on the operating table, she looked up and growled at him "No" and pushed him away. Then she growled "Mama." There was no "coming out of the anesthesia." She wanted out of there. Paul and I had gone to breakfast in the hospital when they paged us. She felt angry and betrayed. For two days she never let us out of her sight. But she began to change after that. She became sweeter. She smiled. She sang. She laughed. We had a new child. Yes, she even slept.

I discovered that my daughter is a classic auditory learner. She had to have audiocassette tapes on to go to sleep. After they ran out, we would hear her retelling them with perfect intonation and voice inflection, even saying "beep" in the right pitch from her storybook tapes. But all of this came AFTER her operation.

(Professionally speaking for a moment here, I believe inner ear problems create subsequent learning and emotional problems. I am researching this hypothesis, but my daughter certainly provides evidence of this. With her ear problems solved, she became a different person. More on this in my next book on learning disabilities.)

Each year I love — and like — her more. A sensitive, caring person, she feels things deeply and knows what is going on inside of others, even when they don't say any words. We are beginning to do seminars together, and we have become so attuned to each other that we can function easily as a unit. We share a passion for children. She loves to baby-sit, as I did as a child. She loves music and is highly gifted in this area, especially piano. A nurturer, she loves lavishing her affection on animals.

Angela and I are both blonde and do "blonde" well together. We can be silly and a perfect parody for "blonde" jokes. But if you look underneath all the "fluff," you will discover two sensitive people; though often silly, we also feel deeply and have a serious side. Angela is my daughter and my friend. She is also my Christmas angel.

The happiest day of my childhood was when my father

awakened me to tell me I had a baby sister. Finally! The doctor had done it right! I was weary of all these brothers. I always assumed my parents had this baby girl for me and me alone. True, my mother had to birth her and get up many nights with her, but by day she was mine. I left my castle in the sky (upstairs) and moved down to her room. I gave up my pretty double bed for a twin bed perched right next to her crib so I could keep an eye on my precious sister. I took Lynelle everywhere with me. I adored her. She was the greatest gift my parents could ever have given me.

As adults, we had our children at the same time, even though I am more than ten years older. This moved us from a relationship in which I cared for her to one in which we were "equals." The bond was unbelievable. So unbelievable that I decided to name my first child after her. I called my baby "Emily Lynelle" the entire time I was pregnant. When I delivered a boy, I went "whoops!" So when I was pregnant with Angela and after we knew she would be a girl, I began to call her "Emily Lynelle." But when Angela was born, we looked at her and said, "She is not Emily Lynelle. She is Angela Elizabeth."

But the strangest thing happens EVERY time we are thinking of going to Minnesota. I begin to call my daughter "Lynelle." It is amazing. It comes out without thinking. I guess a shrink could have a heyday with this. I find it interesting that my daughter brings me back to how I felt for Lynelle all these years. What a blessing to have her as my sister or "sort-of daughter," and my friend. Our worlds are completely different. She is married to a farmer in Minnesota, and I live in the big city. But our oldest children are just a few months apart and our youngest are just ten days apart. God has knit our lives together in a special way.

Confessions of a Travel Terrorist

*G*od keeps giving me opportunities to travel as I serve Him. Up until now, I loved traveling as long as I got to sleep in the car with no responsibilities. But when I have to drive, I get exhausted. Riding in the car is the only time I let go and promptly fall fast asleep.

Back up one scene. Right before God called me to travel, my doctor diagnosed me as having a disorder requiring that I *never* lift anything, or sit for very long—unless I wanted to visit the local hospital. *Great. Now You call me to travel? Good timing.*

Wait. Could it be that I'm supposed to do this in Your Spirit and not my weak flesh?

With my travel history, it's a miracle God even called me to it. Even as a child, I should have realized that I should not try to include travel as part of my destiny. For me, it has been closer to terrorism.

My parents let me go out of town on my own for the first time at age twelve. I went with the band, where we marched in a parade in a small town. Afterward, everybody got to go on one free carnival ride. So I boarded the Octopus with my best friend.

The Octopus resembled a Ferris wheel with cages that spun. Going at a normal speed, the awkward seating angles feel fine because the centrifugal force holds you down. But as our cage reached peak height, the Octopus broke. Did I mention I'm afraid of heights?

We got stranded up there with our necks hanging below our knees for hours. In fact, we stayed up there for so long that our bus left without us. Of course, the band director should have counted kids. But he didn't. At first we giggled. But then we wondered if we would die.

Eventually a fire truck came and hoisted its ladder. I managed to get out of the cage without killing myself. Then I had to climb onto this apparatus, stretching up two miles above the ground.

Once our feet touched ground, we wondered, "How will we get home?" Our bus had disappeared, and we didn't notice anyone looking for us.

Being the shy, reserved person I am, I strutted up to a policeman and asked him to help us. He offered to drive us home — people in small towns are like that sometimes. So we climbed into his car, feeling like hot stuff.

Suddenly, over his radio, came the warning, "ALERT! ALERT! Kidnapping! Two girls kidnapped at the carnival!"

"How exciting! They think someone kidnapped us," we said giggling.

When the police officer pulled into our driveway, we rolled out laughing.

Our parents, out of their minds with fear, had been sure they'd lost us forever. They thought we'd been mutilated. Raped first. Then put up as a freak show. They seemed a touch unhappy about our giggling. They got upset, demanding to know, "How can you act so casual when we've been so upset?"

I turned eighteen before Dad let me leave town again. At that time, he said I could go with my friends on a little excursion to the lake. So a bunch of us barefoot girls drove along happily on our escapade until suddenly the car overheated. (In teenage terms: the engine blew up.)

So Dad had to come get us.

After that he told me, "I don't know if I can let you out again."

But one night I asked permission to drive to the library (on a mission to cruise for guys). Dad agreed. So I drove over to meet my friends, and everybody wanted to go out for Cokes.

Now, in our town, the library was at the top of a huge hill, and the Cokes (and main drag) were downtown—literally DOWN town. We had to go down the hill. Winters in MinneSNOWta bring chilling tales.

I felt confident in my ability to navigate. So off we went. As I drove carefully down the hill, I could see the lights of Dairy Queen beckoning us in the distance. *Let's go. Whoops. A little slip and slide there. Pump those brakes. No problem. Got it under control. DQ, here we come. Whooops! Another icy spot. Pump those brakes. Whoops! Not working so well . . . hey, where did that car come from? Oh, NO!*

In slow motion, our cars found each other's destiny (or density, as George McFly would say). They interlocked.

"Hi, I am so sorry. . . ."

"Oh, hi. . . . Mr. Anderson. . . . Yes, I'm Chet's daughter. Yes, I know you're his boss. . . . Yes, we'll call him. I just know he will be thrilled to hear from us."

"Dad, you won't believe who I *ran into* tonight . . . your boss! No, not exactly at the library. . . ."

So twenty years later when people began asking me to travel and speak, I should have known better. I am not a good risk for it. First came my doctor's words: "Your shoulder cannot handle any travel—unless, of course, you can be sure to have someone carry *all* your things for you."

Yeah. Right. I travel with my children. At first they were too little to carry things and, frankly, I never found a long line of people waiting to carry my stuff for me. Then there's the joke of getting the rental car—trying to stuff in all the luggage, handouts, and books. Funnier yet comes trying to find the place where I am supposed to speak. I have been lost more times than Alice in Wonderland. Then my children chime in with, "Mom, if we were with Dad, *he* wouldn't be lost." At that point I'm sure I can scratch off the gift of encouragement on their "Spiritual Gifts Inventory."

On my first trip, I discovered the airline had lost my luggage, so I arrived with no handouts, no clothes, and sadly, no toothbrush. I learned. My second trip to New York went smoothly. Someone picked me up. It went great. So I got lulled into complacency.

Then came San Francisco. For some reason, I thought this would be my *big break.* I had meetings set up with several publishers. Someone from Focus on the Family had called requesting a tape. *Hey, I might even go there and be discovered! No, this is not a trip to have children along.*

I blew through the savings. I spoke in Los Angeles and left Christopher there with friends. Then I flew Angela to my parents. Good plan.

I had just lost weight. *Might as well frost my hair. Looking good. It always pays to look good if you are about to be discovered. Just this one time.*

After speaking in Los Angeles, I went to see my sister in San Jose. As we headed into the sunset to have dinner in San Francisco near the Bay Bridge, we noted how amazing it was that *two* baseball teams from the area were competing in the World Series. We smiled.

Daddy must be watching the games now. As the cameras pan across the area, will he see us? Hi, Daddy! Yes, your daughters are off to the World Series . . . no, not really . . . just having dinner, Daddy. "What in the world is that rumbling? Hey, Bonnie, I thought you had a decent car. This one shakes like crazy."

My sister grabbed my hand: "This is the *big* one."

"The big what? McDonald's? Come on, Bon, I was hoping for a nicer restaurant. You know, closer to my hotel. Come on, Bon, get this car going. I have a conference to attend. Quit playing around."

Good-bye savings. Good-bye getting discovered. Good-bye new outfit and new "do." I spent the week cleaning up an earthquake. I'd felt the earth move under my feet, but not quite in the way I had hoped.

Next, I took off for Denver. What could possibly happen? You guessed it — the biggest blizzard in years.

After that, off to Oklahoma. I got clobbered without warning by a spring-loaded trunk lid and had to have stitches in my head. I also got a ruptured disc.

Then to Wichita. I decided to drive on this one. Christopher and I had colds. When we got there, we spent the night in our room throwing up. The next morning, I downed seventy-two tablespoons of Pepto Bismol and eighty-seven aspirin, and stumbled out the door to go speak. Someone had slashed my tires.

Now, most sensible people would see these events as "handwriting on the wall." But I knew better. I reminded myself, "God called me to this. This is all the enemy and God is greater than Satan."

It's not easy. I get weary of it. People say, "Oh, you travel all over with your children. What a wonderful life you lead." The truth is, it costs me more to bring my children than I ever make. So we have never gone anywhere like Disneyland. We simply get in the plane, get to the hotel, speak, get back on the plane (or in the car), and come home. But we are together, and we don't get my daily 700 phone calls, and we do try to have fun together. I believe that if I traveled without my children, it would compromise the very message I represent — *which is, be with your children.*

God did bless us the first summer I had after working nineteen straight years as an administrator. He gave us a sixteen-state speaking trip *all* together. Paul drove. We didn't get lost. No natural disasters followed us. We made just enough money to pay for food and lodging and even see some sights along the way. It was a trip of grace, and I will always look back on that with fondest memories. We tried to schedule another for the summer, but nothing worked out. Only a Sovereign God could have known that I would have a broken foot, making it impossible for me to travel in August.

Moral: Don't travel with me unless you want to die

young. Or don't invite me to speak unless you have an exam you're trying to avoid.

Actually, there's more to it than that. It took me a few trips like this to make me realize it doesn't matter so much whether my nails and hair look good. What really matters? Prayer. I involve a whole group of people in my ministry through prayer, and I never go anywhere until I'm bathed in it. Who knows? My friends' prayers have probably held off falling meteors and volcanic eruptions.

Giving
Gifts
of
Time

T hese words "A Gift of Time" bring up many different emotions and memories for me. Time is a very precious commodity and one which I truly treasure. Therefore, because I value time, I consider it something special when I give it away to those I cherish.

I have always worked hard at managing time wisely. I have tried every time system on the market. In time, I began to type up my own time management handouts and copy them. As a principal, I would have an all-day meeting with each teacher during the summer to go through his/her class list, curriculum, prayer, room arrangement, accreditation, field trips, etc. for the upcoming year. This was my "gift of time" I gave to them. They were most appreciative of this focused time, and I felt it was the best investment of my time for the school. We went through a package of forms as we planned.

As time went on, I held time organization sessions for the teachers. My time organization forms for my personal life, church life, and the school began to be part of these sessions. When I resigned as principal, the teachers suggested that I publish these forms. I showed them to several publishers, and they said they were too detailed. I was ready to can the project when a dear friend approached me. Mary Ann said the Lord had given her a burden to help me. She loaned me the money at no interest and without any timetable for repayment, and I published two time organizers myself. One is for anyone to use and the other has additional tabs and can be used for teachers or homeschoolers. The title? *A GIFT OF TIME.*

This led to teaching many sessions on time management. I am a very practical person. I simply am always looking for the most efficient way to do things. What I have discovered is the main challenge for well-meaning Christians is not HOW to prioritize, but how to prioritize our MANY priorities. If we made a list of what we do, rarely are there any activities out of God's will — there are simply too many of them. For example, we can be so busy working in our ministry and thinking we are putting God first in our lives, but in reality we are out of balance. God does not ask us to be so busy working for Him that we neglect our families. All of life is simply a constant struggle for BALANCE.

My time organizer reflects my own struggles in this area. I have a place for the main "to do" list and time slots in the middle of the page. But on the left is a place for prioritizing that list. Which things are for "GOD," which for "MATE," which for "CHILDREN," "HOME," and THEN outside the home. Ouch. Sometimes doing that list hurts because I have not "prioritized my priorities" properly. I don't use that list every day, but I use it to check myself periodically.

As a school principal, I brought my children to work with me until they were school age. While they were with me, I am sure they felt the busyness of my schedule. When we got home, I would take the youngest to bed for twenty minutes and simply hold him or her tight and not take any calls. This would help us to get through the dinner hour. I began to give each child about an hour of my focused attention after dinner. We would play, read, cuddle, have devotions, and talk. This is when I truly found out what was happening with each of my children. I began to call these "Giving Gifts of Time." My children wanted my time more than anything. I believe that all children want their parents' PRESENCE more than just PRESENTS. Giving of ourselves is after all the ultimate gift.

God showed His love for us by giving Himself to us and giving the ultimate gift, His life, so that we might live. God is ALWAYS available for us. We don't need to make an appointment, or to send a fax. And when we call on Him (Jer. 29:12), we never get His voice mail or phone machine. Let's not become so busy that we forget to give back to Him, to talk with Him, read His Word, and simply soak in His presence. Just as the gift of everlasting life is His free gift to everyone who believes on His name, so is His presence always available for us. God is the ultimate GIFT, and He always has TIME for us.

No Pain, No Gain

*N*o pain, no gain." We all hear these words frequently. Ahhh, now I understand why I gain weight. It's all this pain! If I could just get all this pain to go away, I would be thin!

Yet how *do* we get pain to go away?

Pain is a great teacher, but it's one we do not embrace nor do we stand in line to enroll in its classes. It does, however, instruct well when we pay attention.

Physical pain seems to nip at my heels constantly. As I sit here staring at my computer screen, I am contorting my body into a strange position because I have to keep my leg elevated. I broke my foot. I can't use crutches because I have a bad shoulder caused by thoracic outlet syndrome and an injury from a fall. I have heel spurs because this summer in attempt #9,347 to lose weight I was trying to walk three to four miles a day. I have a ruptured disc and a herniated disc from two other accidents for which I must do certain exercises to keep that pain from driving me nuts. But I can't do those exercises because of this broken foot. Let's face it. I'm a mess.

I am still trying to do my church job via wheelchair. My

family is helping at home, and friends are being wonderful to bring meals. But this is getting old. I am a very active person. If my daily activity constituted thinness, move over Twiggy. People who have tried to follow me around in a day have given up. I move constantly. My husband says, "You never stop from the time you get up until you collapse at night." So this inactivity caused by my latest calamity is a real pain in *every* sense.

On top of my physical pain, everyone I know seems to have a comment about this injury because it is easier to see. My other injuries are inside my body, so most people do not realize I am in constant, chronic pain. But now the editorials keep coming: "Boy, what God won't do to you to slow you down. Well, guess He has your attention now. . . ."

Yes, He does have my attention. And when I am not lamenting "Why me? Why now? Why at all?" I am trying to see the blessings in this. I am grateful it didn't happen when I was speaking out of town with one of my children. I am thankful it didn't happen during my eighty-hour VBS week. I am thankful that my husband is on his vacation. He's been great, but I do realize that playing Dr. Kildare this month was not his idea of a vacation. I like doing for others, and having to ask for help is difficult for me. Yes, I know it could have been worse. My brother-in-law, Dennis, is confined to a wheelchair all the time. He constantly praises God. How can he do that?

The night before this happened I wrote in my journal. "Lord, You never cease to amaze me. As I directed the musical at church tonight I became aware that it had nothing to do with me and my efforts, it was YOU. You were doing it through me and the children. I was only the instrument, but it could've been anyone. I was nothing, and You were everything. It was the most glorious feeling. Lord, help me to remember to be nothing and let You be *everything* in my life. Praise You, Jesus." I went to sleep content. I could put every bit of my life on the altar and leave it there.

But once again, "flesh amnesia" has set in. I break my foot and spend the week moaning about everything I can't get done. The only time I cried was when they said it would most likely be casted and I would have to stay off it for at least two months. Wait a minute. Don't they know that I am speaking twenty-three times this month? I can't be in a cast! Get real. Besides, if I can't swim or walk each day, I will weigh 10,438 pounds by the end of all this. I want a quick fix. Can't we put this foot in a microwave or something? I have a life to get on with.

I am still struggling with having to slow down, doing things in God's perfect timing and trusting Him instead of my own energy. I pray that I can pass this test and not be sent another. Let go and let God — it's easier to say than do, isn't it?

God does not take us through the deep waters to drown us, but to cleanse us. What deep waters is God taking you through today? Do you feel drowned or cleansed?

I find comfort in knowing that our great brother, Paul the apostle, knew what pain was. Pleading with the Lord to take away his "thorn in the flesh," Paul heard God answer three times. That answer also speaks to me in my pain — "My grace is sufficient for you, for My power is made perfect in weakness." Paul concludes, "That is why, for Christ's sake I delight in weaknesses. . . . For when I am weak, then I am strong" (2 Cor. 12:9-10).

In the areas where I am strong, it's hard to see the Lord's power in me because, frankly, I don't feel like I need Him all that much. But where I am fragile and utterly dependent on God, He shines brightly through me. It's a lot easier to see sunlight through a window, easily broken, than through a strong, brick wall. Considering the value of my weakness in revealing God's power and presence to the world through me, the wonder is not the areas where I am in pain, but all the places in my life where I'm *not!*

Doing God's Dot-to-Dot

*B*efore a child connects a dot-to-dot picture, he only sees the dots. Our lives are a lot like that. We want God to give us the big picture so we can understand what all these seemingly endless, meaningless dots mean. In fact, I have asked God on many occasions to send me a memo (I'll keep the pink copy, thank you) about what in the world He is doing with my life. But He knows answering prayers like that would not develop my faith. He only allows us to get to the next dot. Then, when looking back, we begin to see what picture He is making with our lives. God only asks that we look to Him for guidance to get to the next dot.

As I look back over the dots of my life, some make sense, others do not. For example, I can connect the dots between having lots of siblings to care for, baby-sitting, elementary education, then generic special education. Add to that Montessori and my current passion for children with learning challenges — particularly Attention Deficit Disorder. It makes sense.

I hurt over the dots that I did not seem to connect well. I was raised in the church, but I did not become a Christian.

No, it was not a Gospel-presenting church. The focus was on good works and liturgy. I got the "good works" part down, but the liturgy left me cold. As a result, I left the church. The side roads I found led me to much pain and disillusionment.

As I said in the beginning, I wish I had become a believer when I was five, met my husband in Bible college. Add to that living happily ever after in full-time ministry. That apparently was not God's plan for my life.

People often assume that because I am in full-time ministry, my life has been like that fairy tale version. I have never kept my past a secret, but people rarely ask about it.

Many of the circumstances in my life seemed overwhelmingly painful for me. Yet if suffering were a competitive sport, I would certainly not qualify for a medal. But in varying degrees, we all know the shocking realization that life frequently fails to obey us and our grand ambitions, or even our little plans. Each of us has experienced the loss of hopes and dreams. And it seems we must face over and over the stunning reality that we live in a desperately fallen world. Life really stinks sometimes.

Yes, life is hard.

But God is good.

And like the angels must have said on Good Friday, *"Sunday's a-comin'!"*

"These Are the Be*st Years of Your Life"

*T*hese are the best years of your life." Did you hear this fewer than 300 bazillion times when you were a child? How did it make you feel? Did anyone ever say it to you when you were a teenager? Were you just as thrilled to hear it then? If you're like me, a relative or teacher made this declaration of doom when you most needed empathy about something like having zits or worrying that you wouldn't make drill team.

At least once when struggling through adolescence, I wondered aloud when it would ever end, and a well-meaning neighbor pronounced that famous death sentence, "These are the best years of your life." I remember my despair as I pondered, "If these are the best, do I really want the rest?"

May I suggest that parents stuff their mouths full of anything nearby when tempted to say those words, because they undermine the seriousness of their children's emotions. Yes, theoretically, childhood should be the best time. Someone takes care of us, and our primary concerns center more around doll houses than mortgage payments, and toy trucks than auto financing.

Yet for many children, childhood is not the finest hour. For example, children with melancholy temperaments take life quite seriously. Being perfectionists, they want to do everything just so. Their standard of perfection means everything and everyone falls short. So they often feel depressed. Most of childhood involves playing and cooperating with other children — not activities in which the melancholy child best relates. For these children, going to a birthday party can be terrifying. Starting a new project or moving into a new classroom can evoke great fear for them. These children cling to their mothers' skirts, wailing, "I don't want to go in there." And the well-meaning parent insists, "What do you mean? Of course you do. It's a *birthday party.* It'll be *fun!*"

In reality, Molly Melancholy already wonders if the children in there will like her. Did she wear the right clothes? Did she bring the right present? Her self-doubts rage in her frightened soul. And then we say to her, "Lighten up — these are the best years of your life. Enjoy them!"

Instead, we need to tell these children, "I believe you will be a content adult." A melancholy child will not turn into an outgoing, bubbly grown-up, but he or she can be content. So we need to give him or her that hope.

For a child who is a little unusual, childhood and teenage years can be grueling. In that season of life, their peers usually base acceptance on shallow criteria. As psychologist James Dobson says, "It is often based on the gold coin of beauty, and the silver coin of intelligence." So if a child is plain or unintelligent, he or she often ends up the target of other children's cruel jokes.

As a school principal, I saw junior high students who had been beaten up emotionally. I would get to know them a little bit and try to encourage them. If they were Christians, I would begin to affirm who they were in Jesus Christ, saying, "I really believe God is doing great things in you. He is building the inside of you, and that will get you through life."

Sometimes I would share with them about a class reunion I attended. Those of us who have endured class reunions know that many of the "in crowd" (their "in-ness" being based on looks, athletics, or cheerleading ability), now experience broken marriages and unfulfilling jobs. They wonder why that varsity sweater won't get them a better job or why that cheerleading experience won't bring them a better marriage. They failed to build the inner character needed to accomplish something. Then we look around at the nerds — the outcasts for whom childhood and teenage years were Nightmare on Adolescence Street. We see people who have what the others strive to achieve. Many have good jobs and great marriages. And we ask, "What happened?"

God developed their insides. Their endurance, hard work, and compassion built from pain helped them build successful lives. As Christians we know that the only true and enduring qualities are those of Jesus Christ . . . love, joy, peace, patience, goodness, kindness, gentleness, faithfulness, and self-control.

As we press through the daily struggles, we need an eternal perspective. When we measure everything from an earthly, worldly, materialistic worldview, we often think the Great Vending Machine in the sky didn't give us the candy bar we wanted in return for our quarter of obedience. But when we view ourselves in terms of what a loving Father is developing in our characters, life begins to take on a deeper meaning.

For believers, these are not the best years of our lives. The best years are yet to come — when we are in heaven, walking in the place where God paves the streets with what we value down here. And better yet, we'll walk and talk with our Lord and Savior, Jesus Christ.

> "I consider that our present sufferings are not worth comparing with the glory that will be revealed in us" (Rom. 8:18).

> "He will wipe every tear from their eyes. There will be no more death or mourning or crying or pain" (Rev. 21:4).

The Snow Is Always Whiter on the Other Side of the Country

*I*n MinneSNOWta, where I grew up, snow falls as early as October 1 and as late as Memorial Day. Once in a while the clouds lose all control and even dump snow on the Fourth of July. That makes it hard to keep the sparklers lit.

Living in all that white can become tedious. I think I understand why the children of Israel got tired of manna. You lose your appreciation for the stuff when you feel like you're buried up to your nose in it. Not only does snow freeze your nose; it also freezes your car door and the engine and the water pump.

Sometimes during college days I walked to school in waist-deep snow because my car felt too drowsy to start. I would trudge from one building to the next wrapped up like Lazarus. Yet the wind still whipped through me.

After I left America's North Pole and headed for the Lone Star State, I enjoyed unloading groceries in January without having to blow dry my fingers to separate them. But after a while, I realized the myth of the greener grass. I began to develop a mutual appreciation for Bing Crosby's preferences, and began to yearn for white Christmases. I didn't need snow all year; but I had to have a white Christmas. So I'd make an annual pilgrimage for a short dose of snow therapy.

Years later when I served as a school principal, I registered snow days at the bottom of my "list." It's not that the cold bothered me so much. It's just that on those days, I had to decide whether our school would stay open or close.

I would arise early and listen to all the weather reports, go out and see it for myself, make the decision, call all the teachers, and start the chain to notify parents. Inevitably some parent would call to ask why I did or did not choose to close. On days we decided to stay open, sometimes most of the teachers couldn't get to work, so the place looked like a one-room schoolhouse with me as the headmaster.

When I resigned as principal, I gleefully announced, "Now I'll thoroughly enjoy snow days, because when they come, I can stay home and play. I won't have to worry about making any decisions."

Our school district has not had one snow day since I resigned five years ago. . . .

I especially love and miss the snow at Christmas. Going home to MinneSNOWta for Christmas will always be a magical experience for me. My mom always decorates the house beautifully. I love to walk in and absorb it before all the siblings and their families arrive. I walk around, look, smell, and feel. My mother is very sensitive to this and tries to let me be the first to arrive.

When we begin to see snow as we drive north, it begins to feed my soul. The snow reflects the Christmas lights. We can't wait to see Grandma and Grandpa's Christmas lights to welcome us HOME. We feel warm inside while it's freezing outside. My mother makes delicious Norwegian cookies, which require an artist's touch. All of this works together to make a most delicious memory. Thus, when there is a REMOTE possibility of a snow day in Dallas, it conjures up all these warm memories. I will admit I do pray for snow each winter in Dallas, but it is rare. But on those rare occasions I can all the "shoulds and oughts" for the day and take my children outside to play in the snow. Then we come in and make a fire and you guessed it. . . . make homemade cookies! I do find myself yearning to move back to the Midwest. My soul yearns for snow.

For me there is nothing more peaceful than watching the world turn white with the beauty of gently falling snow. (Likewise, there is nothing more irritating as well as frightening than trying to get somewhere and a snowstorm keeps you from reaching your goal.) For me, as I watch the snow gently falling to the ground, it reminds me of our Savior's amazing love. By what He did for us on the cross at Calvary, He covers the ugliness of our sins, and washes them white as snow. When I watch a gently falling snow, I feel blanketed in His grace and forgiveness. It reminds me that it is only through His blood that I am purified from all my sins (1 John 1:7), and that all my sins are blotted out forever (Isa. 43:25). How amazing is His grace!

Is This My Life, or Am I Living in a Sitcom?

*W*ords have power; at one extreme they can construct bridges between people, organizations, and countries. At the other, they can build walls that divide and destroy. In between they often confuse. Consider a conversation my family held at the dinner table one night:

Angela: What's a vein?

Christopher: You know . . . like, "Thou shalt not take the name of the Lord thy God in vain."

Before I could begin to unwind that conversation and make sense out of it, our oldest asked Paul, "Dad, what are you playing in the concert tonight?"

Paul: Beethoven. Aba Eben will be there, also.

Christopher: Who is he?

Paul: Israel's minister of defense.

Christopher: You mean he's a football player?

Before I could "fix" that one, my family was already running headlong into round three.

Damon: Dad, aren't you also playing "Anatomy of Peace?"

Angela: Are we having pizza for dinner?

Christopher: No, dummy. PEACE.

Damon: Come on, don't fight about it. Give peace a chance.

Angela: But I don't like peas, I want pizza.

Mom: This is the most amazing digression I have ever heard. What a family. This takes the cake. I'd better go write this one down.

Angela: Are we having cake tonight?

Christopher: Is digression like digestion?

Dad: How can we ever have peace on earth if we who are in one family and speak the same language cannot figure out one conversation?

Angela: So did I ever find out what this vein in my arm does?

Mom: Pass the peas.

The Apostle John speaks of Jesus Christ, saying, "In the beginning was the Word . . . and the Word was God . . . and the Word became flesh and lived among us." Christ was God's perfect Word—His complete communication of Himself to us. But sometimes we run off following some clever digression so we fail to hear what God has spoken clearly through His Son.

"No matter what we feel or think, God is always kinder, greater, better, more beautiful than we ever could have thought," says James Cooke in his book, *Celebration of Grace*. "Even in our very wildest dreams, we have no conception of how good He is. Even His severity toward us is goodness. There's no way we could have something more or better than we already have in Him."

Do you believe God is good? That He loves you infinitely and seeks only your best? If not, stop. Listen. Pay attention to His Word in the flesh—Jesus Christ. He offers salvation, grace, and peace, saying, "My yoke is easy; My burden is light."

How *can* we have peace on earth if one family can't hold a simple, clear conversation? Only through the supernatural power of Christ. The Bible says that one day He will reign on earth as King. Those who have listened to His voice and responded in faith will live forever with no more tears—no more division, destruction, or misunderstandings!

Pride
and
Perspective

I have often said God uses children to teach me the fruit of the Spirit. On the flip side, though, I have also said that from children I continually learn humility. There's nothing like a child to keep me humble. If you feel you have a problem with pride, may I suggest volunteering to work in the children's department?

One Monday morning the teachers said they wanted to have a little breakfast in honor of my thirty-third birthday. Oh, OK, I'll be honest—it was actually my fortieth. Everyone showed up sporting black armbands, and they hung black banners everywhere. It was brutally obnoxious. They did the full forties hype.

For the remainder of the day, the leftover stuff from this bantering I'd received covered my office. One of the fourth-graders came in, scoped out the room, and asked, "Mrs. Capehart, why is all this Over the Hill stuff all over your office?"

In a quiet, melodramatic tone, I said, "Oh, honey. If you can *believe* it, the teachers had a breakfast for me, and they all gave me these. They must think I'm over the hill."

Recognizing I was being facetious, she said, "Well, how old are you?"

"Only forty."

"Ohhh."

I smugly smiled. I *thought* she was thinking, "Oh, I didn't know you were *that* old." But when she opened her mouth, she said, "Ohhhh. I thought you were *much* older."

I was trying to recover from that punch, when she hit me with another one-two: "It must be because you're *fat*, huh?"

I sniffed, "Yeah, that's probably it."

I sat for a moment trying to recover my composure. Then I marched down to the senior pastor's office and requested that this family be excommunicated from our church.

Sometimes to learn humility we have to experience humiliation.

The Bible tells us God gives grace to the humble. Yet, when things happen to humble us, do we embrace them or resent them?

Part of being humble means serving from a heart that expects nothing in return.

Sometimes when I serve, my actions are purely motivated. But at other times, when no one thanks or appreciates me, I feel resentful. Once I decided I wasn't going to do anything unless I knew I had pure motives—that way, when I received no thanks, I would know it was OK. Guess what? I didn't do anything, because I was so busy navel-gazing, analyzing myself to see if I had pure motives.

Part of humility is remembering that God watches and appreciates. Hagar called the Lord, "El Roi—The God Who Sees."

On occasion, God gives me just enough of His blessing to tell me He knows what I do, and He knows my struggles. For example, I was in a public rest room when I ran into a parent I hadn't seen in fifteen years. Her children had graduated from high school. I said hello, and she didn't remember me, but I remembered her. But when she realized who I was, she began to cry and tell me all the blessings her children had received from our school. She told me how they still talk about their positive memories. Now, I had never received any thanks from this woman. She said she didn't even remember me when I first said hello. Yet her three boys' lives had been touched. What an encouragement.

At times I feel deeply hurt over times in my life for which I gave everything but never received thanks. I have to cast these cares upon God continually. Perhaps I will not know until I stand before His throne whether these were truly important.

For fifteen years, I served as the principal of my children's school. I resigned, but we kept our children in the school. The first year, everyone still knew who I was. By the second year, a few new parents had arrived on the scene. At Open House, people asked me questions like, "Are you a new parent?" and "How many years have you been here?"

I had to learn to walk in humility. How quickly we can be forgotten, and how insignificant what we do on earth really is sometimes. Yet, in heaven, we will be surrounded by people whose lives we have touched for eternity.

So when we feel our pride being prickled and poked, and our flesh feels like a porcupine, we have to stop and ask ourselves: Does God see? Yes. Does it really matter that no one is holding Appreciation Night for me? No, it usually doesn't.

After I had served as Director of Christian Education at our church, I resigned because my busy travel and writing schedule made it difficult for me to be there every Sunday. After two years away, I took the job back with the understanding that I couldn't be there every weekend.

In going back to an "old job," I could see how God had been changing me. I no longer felt the need to "prove myself." I simply wanted to go in and quietly serve. I could tell He had supernaturally overhauled me. I felt a deep abiding sense of peace. I had received attractive job offers during that two-year interim, but I knew that God had called me to serve back at Grace.

When we do things in the *Spirit* and not in the *flesh*, it makes all the difference in the world.

Our significance comes not from what we do for others or from our fading accomplishments. We have worth because Someone paid a high price for us, not in dollars and cents, but in blood. The Son of God gave His life for you and me—making us worth more than the whole world.

"The life I live in the body, I live by faith in the Son of God, who loved me and gave Himself for me" (Gal. 2:20).

Was Elvis a Christian?

*A*s an adolescent growing up in the '50s and '60s, I often entertained myself in a fantasy world. If I wasn't dreaming of being in an accident after which Dr. Kildare saved me and fell in love with me, I was rotating romances among the Bonanza boys. By day, I was a good student, model baby-sitter, and helpful daughter. But in my favorite fantasy, by night I was the secret love of Elvis Presley. Every evening he climbed an invisible ladder to my room and sang, "Love Me Tender."

I am now married to a musician, a classical musician at that. Of course, I never told Paul that "Love Me Tender" played a major role in my growing up years. It was my secret, which was never threatened until that fateful day. . . .

Having heard that President Clinton liked Elvis, my child asked me, "Who is Elvis?"

My heart skipped a beat when I heard that name. Trying to distance myself from such "liberalism," I casually replied, "Oh, just a singer who was popular when I was your age." I buried my face in a sack to hide my hyperventilation.

"Was he a Christian, Mom?"

"Maybe," I said, gaining my composure. "If you judged by the end of his life, you would probably think he wasn't. But when I heard him sing Gospel songs, I wondered."

The next time we browsed in a music store, I decided to buy an Elvis tape just to educate my kids. So on that fateful Saturday, I listened to the tape first to be sure it wouldn't warp my children. I was kneading bread, and my kids were *supposed* to be upstairs cleaning their rooms. In that hour, I made the shocking discovery that at mid-life (and supposedly going up on the sanctification scale), I still loved Elvis.

I was rocking away, punching dough, and cleaning the kitchen. Unfortunately, my children quietly observed this phenomenon. They had never heard me play anything other than Christian music, and this was nothing like that.

"Has Mom flipped out? Should we call Dad?" They pondered these questions in their tender, shell-shocked hearts. I guess there's nothing pretty about seeing a middle-aged woman shake her body when there's so much to jiggle. In fact, it might be safe to assume I could have rocked our fair city right off the Richter Scale. As I cavorted into the living room, I saw my children and froze.

"Mom, I don't think Elvis was a Christian. And Mom—are you OK?"

Not wanting to appear *too* defensive, I began to tell them that perhaps, just perhaps, Elvis might have been a believer.

"Of course, only God knows a man's heart. But let's look at a few songs here. 'How Great Thou Art' requires no explanation, right? What about 'Crying in the Chapel'? Now surely only a man broken and contrite before God could sing such a song, right?"

I continued down the list of Elvis' Gospel songs.

"OK, Mom. We get your point. But what about those *other* songs?"

"Like what?" I asked in a high voice, trying to sound innocent.

"The one about the hound dog, and 'Jailhouse Rock' to name a few."

"Oh, those. Well, I think he did those before he came to Christ."

"Mom, do you *really* like these songs?"

"Here, try this one. You'll love it," I said, as I put on that song Elvis had sung to me thousands of times: "Love Me Tender." In a few minutes, my children were snapping their fingers in my face, saying, "Mom, are you in there?"

"Well, did you like it?" I asked eagerly, awakening from my coma.

The looks on their faces told me they didn't. So I continued presenting my defense.

"Look here. 'It's Now or Never.' I think that song means the time is *now* for you to come to know the Lord. And 'Devil in Disguise,' surely refers to Satan being the master of deceit. And 'Return to Sender' . . . yeah, that means when the devil sends his arrows our way, we should just send them back."

I could tell my arguments failed to convince the jury. Finally, I stopped and said, "I don't know if Elvis was a Christian."

And satisfied that I had finally been honest, my children retreated and chose not to report me to their father.

As much as I love Elvis and I hope to be able to praise Jesus with him in heaven, my heart aches as I recognize that the question of his eternal state still remains. If he was a believer, why did his lifestyle reflect such an obsession with self and pleasure? If he wasn't, how could he sing Gospel tunes and hymns with such depth and fervor? It humbles me to realize I am capable of the same hypocrisy—I have the same sinful nature Elvis had, and "there but for the grace of God go I."

That's why we need to pray that God will keep on disciplining us as we give Him our yielded hearts so that we, like Paul, can finish well. Let there be no question, either in our lifetimes or afterward, whether we know Christ. If we were to go on trial for being Christians, let's hope our accusers would find enough evidence to convict us.

"I have fought the good fight, I have finished the race, I

have kept the faith. Now there is in store for me the crown of righteousness, which the Lord, the righteous Judge, will award to me on that day—and not only to me, but also to all who have longed for His appearing" (2 Tim. 4:7-8).

The Pink Lamp

*M*y aunt gave my brother Kevin and his wife the most gaudy pink lamp you've ever seen. Now, don't get me wrong. I love pink. But this thing even overwhelmed *me*. It had a bright pink globe with artificial flowers draping out of it. And it sort of revolved — the kind of lamp they have on dance floors.

My aunt watched him open it, and he managed to get through it without cracking up. But he decided the following Christmas to get even with my other brothers who were there and who walked out of the room graciously before they collapsed in hysteria. Kevin gave this lamp to one of my other brothers at Christmas, and since that time each year, we have passed it around for those "special occasions."

One of my other brothers was away for a few years and missed this family bonding experience. Finally, we were to be together on his birthday. He felt a little embarrassed about being absent for a number of years. So he was trying hard to get back in our good graces.

We all made a big deal about how we had chipped in to

give him a special gift, since we hadn't seen him in several years. He beamed and seemed to feel loved and cherished. But then he opened this horrible lamp with artificial flowers trailing everywhere. Did I mention that he lives in a beautiful home?

I wish I had photographed the priceless look on his face. He didn't know what to say. We were all exclaiming, "Isn't it *wonderful?*" We could tell his mind was searching for something kind to say. Of course, after a few hours, we relieved him of his misery and told him the Legend of the Pink Lamp.

What are the pink lamps in your life? What are the situations that people have given you that you frankly found "worthless." Yet in their eyes, they were "priceless." How do you see beyond the tangible to see the spirit in which it is given?

We might even say God has given us some "pink lamps." At the time, we hardly view them as gifts, but in retrospect we can see the priceless value instead of the "worthless tag" we may have previously put on it.

For example, for years I lamented that I had no sisters. But my mother continuously gave birth to boys. Now I realize that my ten years of fraternity living was the ultimate God-ordained preparation for working on an all-male church staff.

We need some supernatural help in seeing things the way God sees them. When the Prophet Elisha and his servant stood surrounded by the enemy's army, Elisha prayed for his helper. He said, "O Lord, open his eyes so he may see" (2 Kings 6:17). The Lord enabled the servant to see God had surrounded them with His own army, complete with chariots of fire. When confronted with our own pink lamps, we can pray, "O Lord, open my eyes that I may see this from Your perspective." And previously unseen truths will delight us as God joyfully answers our prayer.

Are Children Cheaper by the Dozen?

*A*s I have shared, I thought God's perfect plan for my life would include that I parent 12 children. Instead, He chose for me to *parent* 3 and serve as *principal* for more than 1,000. Yet when I see people doing what I originally wanted to do, I sit up and take notice.

A family in our church, Tommy and Carolyn Klie, have had more than thirty-five foster children in their home (not at the same time), in addition to their four biological children. I stand in awe of what they do and how they do it. I love to watch the transformation in children under their care. The Klies consistently receive the "tough cases," which may include children with cocaine addictions or physical disabilities. Sometimes we teachers feel exhausted after caring for their children in class for only one hour. We ask, "How do they do it day after day?"

I feel convinced that when God calls you to do something, as He has called them, He also provides the grace to accomplish it. Yet this in no way diminishes my respect for their challenge, nor does it lessen my admiration for how well they minister to these children. But God's calling does provide a canopy of grace. And God calls each person to do something for Him in and for His kingdom. The task He assigns perfectly suits our gifts, season of life, and personalities. So why do few people sense "the calling"? Perhaps we see only spiritual vocations, such as serving as missionaries in Africa, as requiring a "call." But directing VBS, serving as a deacon, and yes, caring for the babies in the nursery are all callings. One is not greater than the other. Each can make a significant impact for eternity. We must never measure our ministry's worth by others' standards. The body of Christ needs each of our gifts.

My father-in-law served as a pastor for more than fifty years. Even in his retirement, he continues to amaze us. He visits the sick, donates time to Central American Mission, works at the church, volunteers at Dallas Theological Seminary, and drives the elderly to doctor's appointments. Yet he feels insignificant. I think when we get to heaven we will find out who the true giants of the faith are. They won't necessarily be the names we all recognize, although many of them are giants of the faith. Yet the faithful saints who served quietly in the kingdom day after day, year after year, may well be first in heaven.

I also feel convinced that God makes us different from one another so that we can rightly fulfill our own distinctive function. God consistently demonstrates to us that He creates us to be the garden variety, not canned green beans. My dear friend and prayer accountability partner Jamie Show has seven children whom she homeschools. Years ago, while Jamie envisioned herself more as a career woman, I envisioned myself as a mom-at-home woman. God led us down different paths from what we anticipated; yet both of us believe we are doing what God wants us to do today.

I pray daily for my children that they will desire to be servants, that they will want to serve others and be useful doing God's work. I want them to see modeled before them people who put their lives on the line for the kingdom each day. I want them to know the Klies and of their vital ministry to children. I want them to value their grandparents. I want them to experience ministry both in needy areas of our city and through missionaries we support. My prayer is that the testimony of these truly great people will be a light for my children to follow.

As Henri Fredric Amiel said, "Life is short and we have not too much time for gladdening the hearts of those who are travelling the dark way with us. O, be swift to love! Make haste to be kind!"

Alphabet
Soup

*H*e is A.D.D."
"No, he is L.D."
"Is she T.M.R. or E.M.R.?"
We attach numerous labels to children. I have
used a few myself during the twenty-five years I
have worked with these little ones. Yet children continually
remind me that, even though I can categorize them, God
created each as a unique being.

I teach a seminar titled, "A Look at the Child." First we
consider our *purpose:* to help each child know Jesus Christ
and to be all he or she can for the Lord. A big part of reaching and teaching children involves simply seeing how God
has individually designed them for His purposes. Second,
we look at the *plan* of child development. Each child experiences predictable stages at his or her own pace. Yes, God
even planned for those exhausting toddler years when you
wished your day consisted of doing something less stress-
ful, like air traffic control.

Next, we look at the four *personality* types. In simplified
terms, Sanguine Sally likes to have fun and measures the
success of each situation based on the degree of "fun." We

could describe Melancholy Molly as meticulous and serious; Molly exhibits perfectionistic tendencies. Choleric Carl wants control at any cost. And Phlegmatic Phil naturally serves as a peacemaker. Of course, in actuality, every person's temperament contains a combination of these traits.

Then we look at *perceptual* strengths. This affects the school experience more than anything. All children learn by multi-sensory interaction until age seven. After that, a child learns best when taught at his primary or secondary learning modality strength. When I worked as a principal, if a student experienced learning difficulties, I would "hang out" with her for a while. After she showed me how she learned best, we adapted the curriculum to best fit her learning style. As Dr. Rita Dunn has said so well, "If a child is not learning the way we are teaching him, then perhaps we need to change the way we are teaching him."

Visual learners do well when they can "see it." They like the written word and can read and write the answer. They tend to thrive in traditional learning structures. *Auditory* learners need to hear and "talk about it." In fact, it is the "talking about it" that completes the learning loop for them. *Tactual* learners need to "touch it" and do well with manipulatives. As adults, these people like to "putter" in the garage or kitchen. The *kinesthetic* learner must have body movement. This child's parents often find themselves on a first-name basis with the local hospital's emergency room staff. Teachers most frequently reject this learner, quickly labeling her "A.D.D." I feel concerned about the current trend of labeling each child who is simply a kinesthetic learner as A.D.D. We are medicating children to make our lives easier rather than working with their learning styles.

Finally, we ask "Out of which *part* of the brain is this child most comfortable functioning?" A left-brainer thinks in logical, linear progression. He learns analytically, and he feels most comfortable learning in a quiet environment at a desk or table with bright light. We gear teaching predominantly to this child in most schools.

A right-brain child thinks in whole pictures; she is a global learner. She works best with softer, diffused light, sitting on the floor, in a beanbag chair, or on a bed. She concentrates best with background sound. I have seen many children progress rapidly after we have freed them from sitting quietly at a desk. These children communicate using body language. Often they "scream" the message, yet we educators and parents do not hear their messages. I hurt for these children whom we make to feel "broken" and inadequate simply because they fail to learn the traditional way. How many adults still carry "baggage" from having been labeled or mislabeled? Lingering hurt clouds their self-esteem. God makes each person special and worthy of being treated as a unique creation especially made for His purpose. As I study how individuals learn, and then I see how God leads them, I note that He always matches the vocation to the person. Only humans force everyone into a mold.

In his letter to the Colossians, the Apostle Paul exhorts his readers to clothe themselves with humility (Col. 3:12). Pride causes us to consider our particular learning style as best. Arrogance causes us to rank our own temperaments as superior. Haughtiness causes us to think everyone should operate from the same side of the brain we use.

Paul also tells us to put on a heart of compassion, gentleness, and patience. Having learned that God made us different, we need to celebrate our uniqueness and lovingly encourage others to reach their full potential.

> "I will praise You because I am
> fearfully and wonderfully made;
> Your works are wonderful,
> I know that full well" (Ps. 139:14).

A Whack on the Side of the Head

*M*y friend Roger called me and told me he'd read a wonderful book titled, *A Whack on the Side of the Head*. So I read it too. And I chuckled because it lauded the right-brained, kinesthetic, highly creative person. I write books on right-brained, kinesthetic people, and one piece of information I find consistently in my research is that kinesthetic learners feel miserable—inadequate, broken, and in need of being fixed.

So along comes this book that describes how to become a kinesthetic learner?

Actually, the authors naturally think with highly methodical, analytical, logical, linear perspectives. They needed to include more of the "right brain" in their thinking. So they learned to whack themselves on the side of head, (figuratively speaking), so the creative juices could begin to flow. They had so much joy in discovering this that they wrote a book so other people could whack themselves (figuratively speaking) too. And in this they have done us a great service.

It's good for us to broaden our horizons. We all learn

through the perspective of our learning styles, and yet we usually think everyone else is like us. For every theory ever espoused, when I research it, I've found that it comes through the grid of its originator. No learning style is the cure-all for everyone.

For example, listen to two reading teachers. One will say, "We need to teach reading with phonics." The other will say, "Oh, no, no, no. We need to teach reading with sight words." And wherever I go, parents say they succeeded or failed because of one system or the other. Yet, in reality, phonics is a left-brained, logical, linear way of learning. And using sight words is a right-brained, global, whole-picture way of learning. Both work for different people for different reasons.

Each of us can give a testimonial about how something "worked for us," and that's great. But sometimes we can have a tendency to become dogmatic that our preference will work for everyone else. For example, one family upon finding they enjoy each other's company after throwing out their television can easily begin to insist that every family should throw out their televisions. Or a woman who spends her day writing to politicians may quickly begin to believe that everyone should be equally as committed to doing the same. A man who finds woodworking relaxing can annoy all his friends if he tries to convince them that they too should choose this as a hobby.

Some prefer large churches; others prefer small. Some prefer to serve the Lord in America; others go overseas. Some prefer intellectual-sounding preachers; others prefer to get "riled up." Some prefer a "precept" form of Bible study; others prefer the methods of Bible Study Fellowship. And you know what? They're all correct, if they're seeking to follow God.

For years many of us have read self-help books or been taught "Ten Easy Steps to . . ." this or that, which have prevented us from having to think, pray, ask for wisdom, and wrestle with all the options. We long for life to be black and white—for someone to tell us exactly how to live, down to

the smallest detail, so we won't have to think or struggle.
This would give security — we'd never make mistakes. In
fact, this problem is not new to Christianity. That's probably
why the Apostle Paul spends such a great percentage of his
teaching on legalism. It's a lot easier to tell our kids a blan-
ket, "Dancing is always a sin," than it is to teach them it's
OK in some circumstances and dangerous in others and
how to tell the difference, and how to discern. It's "safer" to
say drinking alcoholic beverages is always a sin than to
trust missionaries in European countries to discern when it
would do more harm than good to reject a glass of cham-
pagne from a kindhearted but unbelieving host.

So where do we draw the line? We draw it at the clear ab-
solutes. Murder, lying, immorality, the Way to the
Father . . . these things are clearly explained in Scripture as
having only one option. But which church to attend, where
to live, how to educate our children — these things require
wisdom.

And God promises His children, "If any of you lacks wisdom, he should ask God, who gives generously to all without finding fault, and it will be given to him" (James 1:5). It
seems that in our effort to conform to Christian codes, we
risk taking the easy way out, we stop thinking, we quit
praying, and, in the process, we leave out God.

Mom, You've Changed

*G*od often uses our own children to teach us humility.

I have always felt a strong camaraderie with my son, Christopher. We've enjoyed reading and discussing books together. We like memorizing Scripture. I've always felt we had this tight relationship. When I resigned from being principal, he wanted me to homeschool him, which intensified the depth of our relationship.

When Christopher was ready to go back to school, I sat down with him and said, "Honey, I know we've always been close. But you're getting ready to be a teenager. You may not always want to be as close to me as you were. Let's just remember to keep the communication lines open. I want you to be honest with me and tell me what you think and feel. And should I *ever* embarrass you, be sure to tell me. OK?"

"Well, Mom, I'm glad you brought this up."

"All right, sweetheart. What is it?"

"Mom, you call everybody sweetheart. It kind of embarrasses me."

So I touched him. "All right. Well, thanks for being honest."

"Well, Mom, that's number two. You touch everybody."

"OK," I whimpered. So I looked at him intently, thinking I would hold this conversation in my eyes.

"That's number three, Mom. When you look intensely, your eyes wiggle."

"Baby—uh, excuse me, Christopher. Let me tell you what—to save time, why don't we make a list of what I'm doing right."

"Good idea, Mom, I'll see if I can come up with one. See ya later, Mom."

Thank you very much, darling. Please pass another piece of humble pie.

When I go to a restaurant or hotel, I take those comment cards seriously. I always complete them. In fact, I even give unsolicited feedback when driving through the line at McDonald's. At the final window, I have been known to say, "May I please speak to the manager for a quick minute if he/she isn't too busy? Thank you . . . Listen, I know you would want to know I found the person in window number one *very* friendly—she deserves your applause. However, I know you would also like to know that your employee in window two didn't even say 'thank you.' " I assume every manager wants to know the status of his or her employees' performance.

My family should be used to this by now. But my husband recently confessed that the reason we rarely eat in restaurants goes beyond mere finance (which he had led me to believe was only the reason). He said he thought waiting two hours for me to complete "feedback forms" bordered on the excessive.

Along these lines, I received another shock to my system this year from my son. I was taking Christopher and a friend to McDonald's. He took me aside and asked, "Mom, if they act really polite, what will you do?"

"Well, son," I promptly replied, "I will give them one of my *Super Wuper Duper* memos to encourage them."

As he turned pale, my smile faded. Then he said, "Mom, maybe just this once, could you let it go?"

"Sure," I said quickly, in an effort to compromise because of his newly found trials in being a preteen.

"And Mom?" he added. "What if they are, you know, *really* rude?"

Seeing the look of terror in his eyes, I held back my urge to be the Junior Holy Spirit for McDonald's and responded, "I will let it go if that will make you feel better. Just this once." In my mind, I knew I could always circle back and do my job after I had delivered the children to their destination.

I have been trying to show him respect for his newly found freedom. He has literally grown a foot this past year, and I am trying to treat him more like a young adult instead of a child. But the reality that I am not the Wonder Woman my son once thought I was is becoming harder to ignore.

He went off to camp for the first time this past summer, so I let him pack his own suitcase. Then, right before it was time for him to leave, I did a perfect "freak out" and began to pack it perfectly. My son later told my husband, "Dad, I just don't understand Mom anymore. I used to think I was just like her, but now I don't understand her sometimes. I think she has really changed."

When he came home, we were talking quietly in his room as I scratched his back. I said, "Christopher, I think maybe I'm beginning to annoy you sometimes, and I want you to know that it is OK if you feel annoyed with me. You have permission to fully own those feelings and to talk about them if you want. I can't promise I will never annoy you again, but if it is something like the McDonald's issue, I am willing to make you less uncomfortable with my behavior."

"Mom, it's so hard," he replied. "I have always loved everything you did, but you have changed. You bug me sometimes."

I answered in my best Spider Woman voice, "Honey, once again you are right out of the child development textbooks. I *should* be bugging you at this age. It is time for you to begin moving away from me. This is totally normal."

"It is?"

"Yes, dear."

He got tears in his eyes, leaned over, and kissed me. "Thanks, Mom. I love you."

As I wrote in his and my journal that night about this new rite of passage, I wrote, "I really want to to enjoy my youngest child [Angela] who *still* thinks I am wonderful. This time is so short-lived, and it may be awhile before I have grandchildren to enjoy—or who enjoy me." The next day, one more rung of reality rotted off the ladder of life for me.

People tell me I am a friendly person. Just as I am the self-appointed Junior Holy Spirit for McDonald's, I am also the self-appointed encourager of all who may feel their jobs are insignificant or mundane. I talk with the garbage collectors and tell them how much I appreciate their work. I know about each member of the gas station attendant's family. I remember how long the guy at 7-11 has been in the country, and he knows my children's names.

I always assumed my children perceived my friendliness as a gift. But as Angela and I ran errands, she heaved a sigh after the lady at the "One Hour Cleaners" counter asked how her piano lessons were coming. Back in the car, she asked, "Mother?" (Now I know I'm in trouble.) "Is there anyone in Dallas, Texas you *don't* know?"

Perhaps I am a bit excessive. Wait. Here comes the postman. I need to run ask how his hemorrhoid surgery went.

"And we . . . are being transformed into His likeness with ever-increasing glory, which comes from the Lord, who is the Spirit" (2 Cor. 3:18).

People change, and we need to let them. Sometimes it's their behavior; sometimes it's their beliefs; sometimes, it's just their perception of reality. It's hard on those around them to adjust, because we're self-centered creatures. We don't like the discomfort of rearranging our worlds. We all resist change.

Yet we need to thank the Lord for change in others' lives, because the ability to choose change is one of the characteristics that makes us uniquely human. Only through internal change can the Lord Jesus remake us into His likeness. Only through change do we grow, mature, and reach the potential God has created in us. We need to serve ourselves a great big helping of patience — that yummy, no calorie fruit of the Spirit, to get us through the process of change in others and in ourselves.

Taming the Teenager

*P*eople ask me frequently, "When is your book on teenagers coming out?" To that I promptly reply, "When I have a few answers . . . don't count on it anytime soon."

I have not always felt this way. Teaching teens and being a principal to teenagers brought joy. I loved them and loved being with them. I found it a happy, harmonious experience. So when did this all change? When my own children hit the teen years running.

Actually, our oldest child's teen years seemed like a walk in the park. This confirmed what I had always thought — that teens were a breeze. "So what's the big deal?" Because I had been surrounded by teens for years, I didn't think I would find it difficult to parent them.

Then reality hit big time. The warnings had been there, but I had missed them.

Our oldest, Damon, has Attention Deficit Disorder. We all experienced so much pain during his childhood years that, by comparison, his teen years have been a cinch. He actually started "coming into his own" during these years, especially after tenth grade. He discovered that his hyperactivity made him a great percussionist. He developed a passion for music which bonded him closely to his father. He began to show sensitivity and care with his siblings. He found the Lord, and church became the anchor in his life. Because he was still a little eccentric (OK, *very* eccentric), he still lacked friends. So the telephone remained quiet. He spent hours in his room listening to music. His only outside activity was church. He wasn't hard to manage.

This past year, our middle son, Christopher, grew nearly twelve inches, and along with that came hormones and an obsession for pizza. His feet grew, his legs extended, and from his ear grew an amazing appendage—the telephone. I receive about thirty calls per day, and my husband, about five. Our son wants that many. So now he answers the telephone *all* the time, or at least during the five-minute intervals when he is not already *on* the phone. Girls and sports have become his sole reason for living. Suddenly, there is music, or what we suspect is supposed to be music, playing in his room. And overnight we have gone from being wise, loving, fair parents to over-the-hill killjoys.

Our precious little girl has suddenly moved from worrying about whether her doll's diaper is wet or not to contemplating the more important issues: "When will I get a bra?" I really thought this would not throw me a curve ball. I am, after all, a calm, rational, trained parent. "Ahhh," as they say. "It's so different when it is *your* children going through this." I struggled. I searched. I prayed. And God has been answering my prayers.

As I felt my son distancing himself from me, God gave me a solution. I would lead a weekly Bible study in our home for his friends. He wasn't too keen on the idea. But knowing a little about business, I told myself, "It's all in how you market things." So I told him, "OK, we can have an hour of Bible study, then thirty minutes to eat, and then you may have an hour for doing what you guys want to do." He heard the last part and agreed. We began. And I must admit, I had some apprehensions.

The first thirty minutes they giggled and looked at each

other self-consciously. Then God intervened. His Spirit moved. And they opened up.

Recently they asked if we could continue our study on an ongoing basis. Praise the Lord! This provides a perfect avenue for me to learn what my son thinks, feels, and believes about music, the Word, staying pure, sex, drugs, and basic Christian values *with* his peers. I had begun to suspect that he was giving me the answers he knew I wanted to hear. But I wanted his convictions.

So I have my first major trial of the teen years behind me . . . now what to do about this bra thing?

To
Own
His
Each

W̶hen I was young, someone gave me a book called *Apples of Gold*. I loved this book. I would read it over and over. Then I went to the store and bought a notebook and began copying my favorite quotes. I did this for years, and I still have this stuffed notebook. I have gone on to fill many more books with my favorite sayings, laced with Scripture passages. In times of trial, these have encouraged me. And to this day, I still love reading quotes and favorite Bible verses.

Sharing with a class of seminary students recently, I told them about a quote that ministered to me just when I needed it. I went on to say that the quotes we collect often reflect our personality and season of life. We must be careful not to make our quotes the quotes for everyone.

Laughing, I said I should write a book of sayings for each personality because, indeed, they would be different. For example, a choleric, strong controlling person who blossoms when given a task to accomplish loves quotes like "When the going gets tough, the tough get going," and "Lead, follow, or get out of the way."

What about the sanguine — the bouncy, bubbly optimist?

She's the kind of person who tends to quote happy, optimistic sayings: "The world looks brighter from behind a smile," or "An optimist sees an opportunity in every calamity; a pessimist sees a calamity in every opportunity," or "When someone says life is hard, ask, 'Compared to what?' "

Then there's the phlegmatic. Phlegmatics are nice, easygoing people. Phil Phleg's favorite quote might be one by Robert Louis Stevenson, who said, "Anyone can carry his burden, however hard, until nightfall; anyone can do his work, however hard, one day; anyone can live sweetly, patiently, lovingly 'til the sun goes down. And this is all that life really is." Phlegmatic people go with the flow, do their best, and are quietly, patiently persevering.

For the melancholy, who may be wallowing in self-pity or feeling overwhelmed by life's inequities, a statement like "Lead, follow, or get out of the way" may cause him to sink further into despair. Melancholy people often get "paralysis of analysis." Because they see the ideal as perfection and they live in a fallen, sinful world, everything and everyone falls short. When we look at most great art and great music, we see the work of a melancholy. He has his own favorite quote: "The optimist lets his kid drive the car; the pessimist won't; the cynic did."

Or the more spiritual, "A Christian should aspire to do the will of God. Nothing more. Nothing less. Nothing else." Or "Faith makes a man a Christian; his life shows he is a Christian; trial confirms him as as a Christian. Death crowns him as a Christian." These help the melancholy see the big picture, the eternal perspective. And because a melancholy enjoys a life of service and sacrifice in many respects, this ministers to this desire and motivates him.

One melancholy husband I know lets his wife signal that he's being too pessimistic. She teases with, "My God is so small, so little and tiny, there's nothing that my God can do."

But this brings us to an important point. We've always heard that the optimist sees a glass of water as half-full, as opposed to the pessimist who sees it as half-empty. The optimistic viewpoint is then lauded as the correct perspective. Indeed, that conclusion alone has been seen through a personality grid.

When I spoke with those seminary students, one young man told me he was genuinely relieved to hear that it's OK to see things the way he sees them. We need to find what ministers to us the way God made us. Find a quote that ministers to you, and write it in the little box that's left for you. And remember — this is your quote for what you need. No one else's favorite sayings have to be yours. You are God's unique design.

```
┌─────────────────────────────────────────────┐
│                                             │
│                                             │
│                                             │
│                                             │
│                                             │
└─────────────────────────────────────────────┘
```

"For we are God's workmanship, created in Christ Jesus to do good works, which God prepared in advance for us to do" (Eph. 2:10). The Greek word for "workmanship" means "poem." I love that! In creating each of us, God has written a love poem to Himself. Some may be epic odes — others just might be limericks.

A line in a children's song goes like this: "And I just thank You, Father, for making me me." God rejoices in how He made us, saying (a loose paraphrase of Gen. 1:31), "I did GOOOOOOOD!" Shouldn't we let ourselves enjoy His creation just a teeny bit?

"For Thou didst form my inward parts
Thou didst weave me in my mother's womb.
I will give thanks to Thee,
for I am fearfully and wonderfully made" (Ps. 139:13-14).

"As it is, there are many parts, but one body. The eye cannot say to the hand, 'I don't need you!' And the head cannot say to the feet, 'I don't need you!' " (1 Cor. 12:20-21)

Partnership Polarities

*W*hat we like to do on vacation reveals a lot about us.

When my husband and I married, we had no money. (Nothing much has changed on that score.) We spent our week-long belated honeymoon at a friend's farm in Arkansas. It had no electricity. We had to go to sleep when the sun went down and rise with the roosters. We were out in the middle of the boonies, so there was no form of entertainment for miles around us. We were not bored with each other, however.

I packed a pile of books, and people laughed. They told my laid-back husband, "Jody will last two days at the max, and then you'll have to get her out of there because she'll go crazy."

The reality? I was totally content. We had time to talk, read, relax, and . . . I wasn't ready to leave. My husband, on the other hand, after a few days, climbed the walls and then the ceiling.

Now, if you observed us in our home, you would peg me the active one and Paul passive. I live by my "to do" list. I rewrite my schedule sometimes several times at night. Often I even add something to the list that I've accomplished so I can have the pleasure of crossing it out. I putter around, clean up, answer the phone, and do three things at once. I have not yet learned what my friends tell me — that "No" is a complete sentence. Paul reads and watches television while I busy myself around him.

When we go on vacation, an invisible switch must flip inside both of us. We fall into opposite roles. I throw away my schedule. I don't want to be anywhere at any specific time. Paul becomes the opposite. He's so used to me planning everything that he longs for the structure I provide.

I stay up all night getting ready for vacation, packing everyone, finishing up last-minute duties, and starting on the following month's work. I leave everything by the front door. Paul rises at 5 A.M., packs the car, and throws me into the front seat with a pillow. I fall asleep before we leave the driveway, after giving strict orders that everyone must leave me alone and awaken me only for meals. On a trip, Paul takes charge, navigates perfectly, and drives like a Type A.

At home, I'm driven; on vacation, I enjoy being driven. When I take a vacation, I become a new person. I watch sunsets, smell honeysuckle, enjoy the feeling of sand between my toes, and ask myself why I don't remember to do this day-in and day-out. But when I get back into my routine and the phone rings continually, the demands and deadlines begin to dictate my priorities, and it's an effort to make myself stop and appreciate the smell of good, Colombian coffee.

But whether at home or on vacation, Paul and I have opposite temperaments.

Because most people marry their opposites, I have to believe this demonstrates God's plan. He shows us His graces while He sends us to His great character-building school. In fact, I believe He has enrolled many of us in graduate courses. Personally, I'd like to know where I can take speed-learning classes.

If this is such a great plan, why does this polarity exist in our partnerships?

Perhaps God wants us to complement each other; in the process, He wants us to love unconditionally, to accept each other, and to nurture each other. Our opposites soften our edges.

Yet there are times it can be a trial. One author has titled his book *Opposites Attack*. The very things that attracted us often become the things we spend the rest of our marriages trying to "fix." For example, Paul considered it cute that I decorated so much for holidays. He'd never met anyone who got so excited about special events. But after we married, he asked me, "You're not really going to keep doing that, are you?"

When we met, I thought his easygoing temperament was great. Later, I wanted him to show more initiative.

I received a call from a meeting planner for a large conference asking me to speak on "Wives' Expectations of Their Husbands." They scheduled me for the last session on the last day of the conference. I figured no one would stick around for that time slot. So I planned to meet with five women who would come and complain about their husbands. We'd cry and pray together; then we'd all go home and that would be the end. I prepared a few pink handouts.

Next, I discovered the conference director had scheduled me to speak in the auditorium, and I thought, "Oh, crud. Huge room. We'll have to take our little group and go sit together in the front." But when I walked in, the place overflowed with people — including equal numbers of men and women. I asked, "Why are y'all here?"

To hear about, "Wives' Expectations of Their Husbands."

"You ARE? You men too?"

"Yes. We really want to know what our wives expect." Talk about revealing a need.

I talk to couples frequently, and their most consistent complaints relate to being opposites. Men say, "I felt attracted to her because I'm not a talker. I found her funny and entertaining. But now she never shuts up." Or their wives say, "He attracted me with his strong silence. I was going to bring him out. In our courtship, I could get him to talk, but after we married, he clammed up again."

Another says, "I felt attracted to her because she couldn't get enough kissing; I thought she'd be hot. But now on the rare occasion when she says, 'I don't have a headache,' I say, 'I've been waiting to hear that for six weeks.'"

It's a downward spiral. One becomes angry about something. The other withdraws. The first reacts by becoming even more aggressive. So the other retreats further.

We can say, "In the spirit of compromise, I'd like *you* to change." But those changes aren't likely to happen.

So first, we have to remember our commitment. We live in a generation of speed that taps its fingers impatiently while waiting for microwave dinners to heat. Almost every family goes through seasons with sick kids and mounting bills when everyone grates on each other. During those times, walking out would be the easy option. But we don't abandon each other or our children, because we've decided we're committed.

Once we agree we're committed, our only alternative is to celebrate the differences — to meet at the walls that divide us and start tearing them down.

One common expectation is that the man rules the roost. But what happens when an extroverted woman marries an introverted man, which is often the case? When an aggressive female lives with a passive male, both spouses can fear that their biblical roles have crossed. This can heighten the tension over personality traits. But submission is not a role, it's an attitude. An extroverted woman can have a submissive attitude; an introverted man can show strong, loving headship — while neither has to overhaul his or her God-given personality.

Both partners should assess their strengths and weaknesses, and use strengths to mutual advantage. Wives are better at many things than their husbands, and vice versa. As rational human beings, then, we ask "Who is best equipped to handle this task?" For example, if the wife drives her husband nuts with details, she may also be better at balancing the checkbook. If so, let her handle it.

If the husband's laid-back attitude makes him cooler in tense situations, perhaps he is better equipped to handle a confrontation with the telephone company.

We appreciate our differences more when we can use them to our mutual advantage. God made us different for His purpose. Let's cherish those differences.

Nothing brings out contrasts in us more than parenting. My husband and I agree on biblical issues and parenting theory. Yet our styles often reflect our personalities. So we spend hours discussing how to handle our children so they receive consistent messages from us. Now we jokingly acknowledge that there's only one reason why our children have not been abused — we rarely feel totally angry at the same time. When one of us lunges forward, ready to ground a child for life, the other steps in, making a case for a little forbearance. And likewise, when the other is ready to terminate the child's existence, the other defends a more "chilled out" approach.

We need each other!

For us, one of the glorious discoveries in taking years of endless discussions, compromises, and a commitment to loving and accepting one another is that we have *both* changed. We have met at the wall so many times in our desire to tear it down that we've even crossed the line that divides us. We joke that by the time we've been married fifty years, Paul will be like me and I will be like Paul.

Well, maybe not. . . .

Paul and I talk often about how our parents are opposites. His father is a serious thinker and a servant for Christ. His mother loves the Lord with a more outgoing and amusing approach. Her best line: "I never let my Christian morals keep me from doing what is right." My father is funny and loves everybody. My mom is more introspective and expresses her care for others through giving. Family gatherings may find our parents working in the kitchen pondering the deeper issues of life. Why does God have us marry our opposites? I believe to help us find the essence of unconditional love and to balance the extremes in our natures. Most of life is a series of compromises, and perhaps that is what achieving peace on earth is all about.

Foot in Mouth Disease, or What Does *a* Real Cowboy Do?

hen I broke my foot this year, people wondered if I had sustained the injury by simply biting down too hard on it. After all, my mouth is usually where my foot ends up. Perhaps an entire book could be written on all the faux pas of my life. It rarely occurs to me that I don't have to say everything on my mind.

At a wedding I was talking with a man about publishing. He asked me why I hadn't written for a certain publisher. I answered his question, and as the conversation continued, I asked him why he had such a passion for this particular publishing house. Everyone around us looked horror stricken. Then a friend gently kicked me.

"I am the president," he explained.

Everyone, of course, knew that but me. I should have, but I rarely pay attention to details such as titles.

This man remarked that it was refreshing to meet someone who didn't know *who* and *what* he was. The senior pastor, in sheer delight, began to tell him about all the *other* people I didn't know. (Unfortunately, I could tell many stories on myself here, but I will spare myself total humiliation, and only retell a few.)

There was the time I asked a man who had his children in our school and for whom half of Dallas is named if he thought he could afford private school tuition for his four children. I am sure he laughed all the way to his DeLorean.

Another time I was interviewing a couple who wanted to put their children in the school.

"And what do you do for a living?" I asked the father.

"I'm a Cowboy."

"A Cowboy? I have never met a *real* Cowboy. What do you do these days? I mean, it's not like in the movies, is it?"

"No Ma'am. I play for the Dallas Cowboys."

"Oh . . . are you the one who played in all those Superbowl games?"

"Yes."

"Oh. . . . "

And then there was the time back in my youth when I took my students to compete in the Special Olympics. I kept hearing the name of a famous athlete who had come to support the Olympics by bringing celebrity status. I saw his name everywhere, but I had no idea who he was.

Now, as a single lady, I usually noticed attractive men, and I saw one. *Oh, he's pretty good looking. Come on kids, let's meander over toward this guy.* He and I chatted as we walked the track. *Whoops. He's wearing a wedding band—so let's just make polite chatter.*

"Say do you know who this so-and-so is?" I asked innocently. "I have never heard of him, but he must be *some big deal.*"

"Yes, he must," my new friend replied. As we turned the corner, the crowd went berserk—looking in our direction. I wondered why.

"He must be around here somewhere." I was looking around. "Why is everyone looking over here? (Then the moment of harsh reality.) Oh, no . . . are you. . . . let me guess. . . ."

He smiled and waved to the crowd, winked at me, and walked to the platform.

My son says that no book would be complete without *the* football story. A Cowboy who put his child in my school donated a *real* Dallas Cowboys football with *all* the signatures of *all* the guys who had played in the Superbowl that year. It was *the* raffle item at our annual fundraiser. I didn't buy any tickets — what in the world would I do with a football? Get real.

So when my name was announced as the winner, I was most surprised.

"I didn't enter it!"

"But we entered for you," stated the football player. "I bought 100 tickets in your name. You won."

"Now come on, I appreciate the thought but what in the world would I ever do with a football?"

At that point, my husband quickly cupped his hand over my mouth and finally exclaimed, "Thank you very much!"

Years later, I remembered I still had that football, so I told my son about it.

He nearly passed out. He promptly took over odd jobs so he could earn enough money to purchase a glass case to "protect" this, the greatest treasure of the universe. He loves to tell the story about his mother who won a Dallas Cowboy Superbowl football and didn't even want it.

But who would believe such a story?

I know the Apostle Paul can empathize with me. When he appeared before the religious leaders to make his defense for being falsely accused, the high priest ordered those standing near him to strike him on the mouth. He responded by yelling, "God will strike you, you whitewashed wall!"

Those standing near him asked with astonishment, "Do you dare to insult God's high priest?"

Paul immediately apologized, explaining, "I was not aware that he was high priest, for it is written, 'You shall not speak evil of a ruler of your people.' "

Which being interpreted means, "Oops."

Paul demonstrated that even great and godly leaders make mistakes. And even though the high priest had done wrong, Paul immediately and publicly apologized for his own actions. I hope we are all quick to do the same.

Cleanliness Is Next to Compulsiveness

*M*y husband knows one great way to make me happy: spray Lysol around the house. It makes me think something is *clean*. I will not go so far as to label myself "compulsive," but I certainly enjoy life more when everything shines and looks organized. I like having things clean. My family misinterprets this. They think I love to clean. I understand the difference. No, I don't wash my hands twenty times an hour; I just like having everything in order.

We usually marry our opposites, right? Well, I like things to be in perfect order in converse proportion to my husband's desire to want things out of order. When I first saw his home back when we called ourselves "just friends," I said to myself, "Good thing I do not plan to marry this guy. I could never stand it." Remember the old adage, "Never say never"? (So I am trying this one out: I *never* want to be thin. Hasn't worked so far. . . .)

I work hard to pass along my standards of *order* to my children. At age three, Christopher said, "I love organizing." I took this as a sign of budding genius and worked hard to perfect this already advanced character trait. As I look at his room now that he has become a sports fan, I'm not so sure. But I do believe that when he lives by himself, his apartment will reflect my hard work and his basic nature.

Angela — well, there's another story. Any neatness she exhibits has come purely through training. But she likes to please, so I am capitalizing on that to try to build in her habits which, hopefully, she will use later.

As if my vendetta against dirt weren't enough, did I mention that my friends call me a packrat? This malady commonly exhibits itself in teachers of children. We see everything as having potential to *be* something, so we figure we should save it. Now, this desire to save everything and my desire for organization clash on occasion. To the same degree that I love being creative and making messes, I also love having everything ordered, labeled, and alphabetized. This causes me internal turmoil. I am a victim of my own polarities. I have met the enemy and I am "it."

I share this incongruity in common with my creative younger sister, Lynelle. She runs a business growing flowers, drying them, and making exquisite arrangements. Sometimes she feels she will drown in the messiness of making things pretty.

As the old Shaker hymn says, " 'Tis the gift to be simple, 'tis the gift to be free, 'tis the gift to come down where you ought to be." I often pray, "Lord, teach me to let go of the things I don't need to save. I don't need to save *every* photo, *every* project my children have created, and *every* cute thing that could possibly be something someday. . . ." This isn't easy for me. I clean out, throw out, give away, and feel good and free; and then, little by little, things pile up again.

"De-accumulate!" exhorts Richard Foster in *Celebration of Discipline*. "Masses of things that are not needed complicate life. They must be sorted and stored and dusted and re-sorted and re-sorted *ad nauseam*. Most of us could get rid of half our possessions without any serious sacrifice. We would do well to follow the counsel of Thoreau: 'Simplify, simplify.' "

For Lent, I'm Giving Up Girl Scout Cookies

The first time I served on an all-male-but-me board, I was with a bunch of long-faced conservatives with an attitude of, "We take our ministry seriously." Unspoken rule: "We don't smile." One day each took his turn around the table sharing his key spiritual goal for the year:

"I want to read my Bible seventy-two hours a day."

"I plan to memorize the New Testament this week."

"I will fast twenty-nine days a month, except in February."

Then my turn came. I had been so out-spiritualized, I couldn't take it. So I quietly shared, "My goal is to get my body's temple in such great shape that *Sports Illustrated* will ask me to be on the cover of the swimsuit edition."

Actually, I was almost serious. I do want to lose the weight I've never dropped after having Angela, so I can quit saying, "I just had a baby." I have this fear of being nominated for the "Good Year Blimp Poster Child." And I worry that I will greet guests at Angela's wedding, mumbling, "Well, you know, I just had a baby," as I stuff my face full of wedding cake.

If reading diet books made you thin, I would be Twiggy. It's not knowledge that makes me overweight; it's feelings. Carrots and water don't fill my emotional void like chocolate and Coke.

It never fails. Right after I finish devouring a huge Thanksgiving dinner, I feel positive I will be able to go on the greatest diet of all times. I will even breeze through all the holiday parties, because I am going to lose ten pounds before Christmas.

I am so sure of it on Thanksgiving Day, that I'm cocky in my confidence that I will obtain this reachable goal. But at about seven or eight that evening, amnesia sets in and I scarf down another piece of pumpkin pie topped with whipped cream. Why offend Mom, who lovingly prepared this feast? I go for another piece of chocolate too.

So it is, after trashing out all of December, as I sit between Christmas and New Year's, I think, "Ah, it's almost New Year's. This will be a fresh start. I will only drink water. I will give up Coke. I will even give up chocolate. I will crave celery. This will be the year during which I can use my string bikini for something other than my son's science project on kites." On New Year's Eve, when I write out my goals for the new year, I'm confident this will be the year Revlon will say, "Move over Cover Girl."

The next morning, on New Year's, I think, "This is a special day. Wouldn't it be fun to make bacon and waffles for breakfast?" And about 6 o'clock that evening, as I'm in total Coke withdrawal, I am sure I was in a coma when I wrote those stupid, idiotic goals. So I flick on the switch to the conveyor belt, and the food starts rolling into my mouth.

But after that, I repent and once again start working on my goals.

Then comes my son's birthday on January 13. A little piece of birthday cake won't hurt.

Then my birthday rolls around in February . . . and then Valentine's Day . . . and pretty soon, I'm completely back to my old ways. At the end of February, I repent once again. I resolve to mend my ways, because now it's time to give up something for Lent. My church doesn't observe Lent in the traditional sense, but I decide, in a move of ecumenical oneness, that I will hold my own private observance.

So I lay my chocolate and Coke on the altar. I say, "Lord, this is what I'm giving up for You for Lent." And as I am piously praying over this, I hear a knock on the door. I open it to find a precious, wide-eyed child dressed in a green uniform. She asks, "Would you like to buy some of my cookies?"

Being the noble and generous person I am, I say, "Of course, I will buy some cookies to support your cause." I tell the Lord, "I know this will be OK because I've put it on the altar. I can have Girl Scout cookies in the house, and they certainly won't tempt me. I am giving them up for You." And so, because I naturally want to support my local non-profit kids' organization, I graciously buy 300 boxes.

Now, the problem is, the cookies don't arrive until eight months later. And by then, Lent is over. Good Year Blimp, here I come!

A friend told me recently, "One of the things I admire about you is that you don't seem that uptight about your weight." Was that supposed to be a compliment?

The Apostle Paul wrote, "I do not understand what I do. For what I want to do I do not do, but what I hate I do. And if I do what I do not want to do, I agree that the law is good. As it is, it is no longer I myself who do it, but it is sin living in me. I know that nothing good lives in me, that is, in my sinful nature. For I have the desire to do what is good, but I cannot carry it out. For what I do is not the good I want to do; no, the evil I do not want to do—this I keep on doing" (Rom. 7:15-20).

I've heard it suggested that the Apostle Paul's thorn in the flesh was an eye problem. Could be, but I personally think his thorn in the flesh was a weight problem. I mean, think about it. Wasn't it *convenient* that he was a tentmaker?

No matter. I fully understand Paul's discourse on wanting so badly to be good. The older I get, the more I know that "nothing good lives in me, that is, in my sinful nature."

Learning to struggle with all His energy instead of struggling with my own puny energy is one of God's biggest ongoing works in my life (Col. 1:29). It's so much easier to just give in!

The Scent of
a Christian

*W*hen I became a Christian, I thought I needed to learn the behavior patterns and language of a new subculture. These actions and passwords would show that I was a card carrying member of The Club. Frankly, some of them still bother me because they are the very words that worked like a repellent to keep me out of The Club before I finally joined.

For example, in my quest to find what was missing, I attended a fundamentalist church. Those nice, friendly people kept asking, "Are you saved?"

I wasn't sure from what I was supposed to be saved . . . perhaps from them.

They told me Jesus saves. Saves what? Pennies? Savings bonds? What?

So I didn't go back.

After I did get saved from hell, people took me aside several times and tried to direct me away from potential land mines that awaited the naive such as me. The greatest shock hit below my educational belt: "Don't use the word, 'Montessori.' Christians don't use the word 'Montessori.' "

Where was that in the Bible? Hallucinations 7:14?

I wanted to conform to the culture. But I had three degrees in Montessori, so this was going to be tough. I threw out the healthy Montessori apple with the rotten core. I changed every bit of the school's curriculum to a strict system of fundamentalist Christian textbooks, all of which were deemed acceptable by the conservatives I was trying to attract to the school.

But soon I discovered that lessons taught only on paper failed for some students. So I began to sneak in some of my Montessori equipment and supplement the curriculum. I just never mentioned the M-word. Finally, I wrote curriculum for our school, which blended both approaches.

As Kenneth Gaebelein has said, "All truth is God's truth." "Two plus two equals four" is true in both the spiritual and non-spiritual worlds. If it's truth, it's God's truth. If my equipment helped me teach a principle that did not violate God's truth, I used it.

I began to understand why Christians steered away from Montessori—because of the humanistic approach to teaching how the world was created. So I left out that part. As I grew in confidence as a Christian and prayed for wisdom, the Lord granted me the vision to see how to blend the good part of Montessori with Christianity.

Sometimes you know you have a balanced approach when people from both extremes attack you. I would attend Christian education conferences and hear, "Jody, we hear you do *Montessori* at your school." (Translation: How could you? You pagan!) Then I would go to Montessori conferences and hear, "Come on, Jody. We hear you are now teaching *religion* at your school." (Translation: How could you? You Jesus freak!)

About the time I learned to refrain from using certain educational buzzwords, I also discovered I needed to be careful about some other fine points of my behavior—for example, my choice of perfume.

It all goes back to one of my earlier teachers. She would walk up and down the aisles checking our work. I will never forget her—not because she was a great teacher, but because she had such nauseating B.O. I felt sick nearly every time she came near me. Then and there I decided that one of the most important qualities in a teacher is to smell good.

My first year of teaching, I taught severely handicapped children. They probably had little awareness of anything. Yet, every morning after I would arise, dress, and put on earrings to match my outfits, I would splash myself with perfume. A day never passed when I didn't think, "I want them to enjoy seeing me and being near me. I want them to feel good when I'm around them, and, yes, may the fragrance of my presence be a pleasant memory."

Unfortunately, those perfumes were Passion and Obsession. Yes, these sounded carnal and worldly, yet I really thought they smelled good. One day I thought, "Real Christians shouldn't wear pagan-sounding perfumes."

People don't always like being "should-upon," so my husband and I were discussing this vitally important spiritual issue one day and came upon a solution: "We should come up with some Christian names for perfume for those of us who like to smell good but don't want to offend anyone by wearing a godless-sounding scent."

We started coming up with good Christian names like Confession, Submission, Repentance, In the Garden, Forbidden Fragrance, and Mary Magdalene. My husband suggested a cologne line for men called "The Road to Damascus ... for the man who wants to be transformed." Think the world is ready?

Meanwhile, back to school. I decided I could teach some Montessori. And it was OK to wear Obsession. In the process of sorting through these issues, I discovered how easy it is to put limitations on the Christian life that God never intended.

Some churchgoers have developed standards about what real Christians do or don't do. Real Christians don't go to movies. Or real Christians only go to G-rated movies. Real Christians don't drink any alcohol of any kind. Real Christians only sing hymns. Or real Christians only sing praise choruses. Real Christians vote Republican. Real

Christians have a daily quiet time by 6 A.M. Real Christians homeschool their children. Or real Christians send their children to a Christian school. Or real Christians send their kids to public school as a witness. The problem with all these ideas is that they have created an external, measurable standard by which we can easily judge each other.

How much more joyful the body of Christ would be if we all asked the Lord to purge our minds of the obsession to add unnecessary, ungodly requirements to what Jesus has already completed.

They will know we are real Christians by our love.

"Now these three remain: faith, hope and love. But the greatest of these is love" (1 Cor. 13:13).

Shrink-
wrapped

I feel guilty. I had a happy childhood, but I'm
keeping that fact to myself. A lot of people just
assume that everyone had a horrible growing-
up experience, asking, "How bad was yours?"
First it was popular to say, "I can't get my act
together because of this or that." Next people told me, "I
came from a dysfunctional home." Now they just ask,
"Who's *your* therapist?"

So I hesitate to confide that I've talked to a counselor, because some people wear "dysfunctional" like an award. I
don't want anyone to accuse me of bragging. Nevertheless,
I've needed to see Mark, a therapist, several times over the
years. Actually, I could afford only three sessions. My money ran out before my problems did.

I offered him a reasonable solution—I would provide
child care for his children between 3 and 4 A.M. daily (my
only uncommitted time slot). For some reason, my schedule
didn't quite fit with his baby-sitting needs. But my barter
clued him in on my most immediate need—he told me I
needed to establish some boundaries.

As I've already said, I grew up in a home with seven siblings. Did I mention we shared one bathroom? Everyone left the door open when they "took care of business" so others could come in and out. We thought that was normal. Things were always pretty loose at our house. As a grown-up, I feel close to each of my siblings, and I love going home to see my parents. Yet I find some aspects of going home painful.

For example, no one in my family makes definite plans. Everything can change 3,000 times a day. My kind of personality moves into situations ahead of time. I want to mentally enter a scenario before I actually live it. The front side of this is that I'm organized; the back side is that I'm inflexible. So going home may push these buttons. I try to imagine myself as a rag doll, not reacting to all this. But in reality I find myself going nuts when there is no structure or schedule.

I live off my time organizer. Unfortunately, I never remember to add time for buildings burning, children getting ear infections, dogs pooping on carpets, and flat tires. I tend to pray, "Lord, I'll do whatever You want me to do to-day—but could You make sure the unexpected interruptions only happen between 4 and 5 A.M.? Have Thine own way, as long as it fits my plans."

I have it backward. I need to write my schedule *after* I pray, and even then, write only in pencil, realizing I may need to erase it and change it to meet His plan for my day. My life, my children, my plans, and precious moments with Him must come His way, in His time. Often, I find myself questioning God's ability to make things happen at the right time. I have wished I could FAX Him a copy of my schedule, so He can deliver the things I want *when* I want them. That's like asking, "How can I better help Him to know His will for my life?"

I should have figured out years ago that things rarely happen as I plan them. My small children never said cute, adorable things when I had my pen poised, ready to write in their baby books. When I did have my pencil ready to write down the pearls as they rolled off my son's lips, he stared blankly at me. Of course, after I buckled him in his car seat, and tore down the expressway, or ran errands with no writing utensils in sight, he became a genius.

I felt sure I would never forget his adorable remarks. But a few hours later, I would try to repeat them to some neighbor who was convinced her kids cornered the cuteness market. I'd say, "Christopher said the *funniest* thing today!" Then she'd stand waiting with a doubtful but expectant look on her face while my memory took a vacation.

I have noticed a similar pattern when I sit to write. In the middle of a symphony, I get great book ideas. But as soon as I plop myself in front of a computer, my mind goes as blank as the screen. I pray, "Come on, Lord. You remember those ideas You gave me, don't You? Come on, FAX them down. I'm ready."

I need to become more flexible, but part of having time to be available means learning to put some limits on interruptions by setting up boundaries.

With my children, I have worked hard to establish boundaries. I give each of them an appointment at night. They have one hour with me individually. Some may think it sounds cold to make an appointment with your kids, but to us it's a great gift. My children know that no matter what kind of day they're having, they have that standing appointment during which they will have my undivided attention. It's their time—they call the shots in terms of what we share. I call the shots in terms of checking schoolwork and signing papers. But then we talk, read, snuggle, and scratch backs. That's when I really find out what's going on in their lives.

It provides security for them, and it provides structure for me. If I didn't set aside that time, blocking it out on a to-do list, I know I would fill it up with laundry, phone calls, and paperwork.

Then there's life at the office. Where do my boundaries fit in there? If I make myself available all day, all my time goes to others. Some days other people's problems consume my whole day. Then I head home with two briefcases full of work, praying, "Lord, surely it isn't Your plan for me to be up until 3 A.M. every night/morning."

For example, back in my school principal days, I would have a big report due and I'd be sitting at my desk nursing a migraine headache. A teacher would enter.

"I can't find the glue. Will you help me find it?"

"I'm really busy."

"But I can't find it."

At that point I would quell the urge to snap, "It's on the third shelf. I've devised this clever system. The place that's marked G-L-U-E—that's where the glue is. It took a college degree to think up that one."

People would visit my office more than they should. Finally, I asked some of the teachers to tell me why and to help me establish a balance between giving them my time and getting my own work done.

One said, "I used to sit in my classroom and think of reasons to go to your office."

"Why?"

"Because I liked seeing you. I came out with a charge."

"Even if I had a migraine and a report due?"

"Then I'd probably feel guilty, but mainly I'd get a charge."

Speaking of charge, I wondered if I should start charging for my time: "See Jody Capehart for your entertainment needs."

So I go to Mark's office. I'm in pain, I'm overworked, and I'm tired. I don't like it. I realize I've been putting up walls to shut out relationships. I'm nonverbally saying, "Leave me alone." People perceive me as an extrovert who always has a joke, but sometimes I'm dying to be by myself with things in order and quiet. So I tell Mark, "People perceive me this way. What do I do?"

"Set boundaries."

"OK, Mark. Let's role-play."

"Sure, Jody."

Knock, knock.

Jody: Yes? (No smile.)

Teacher: Hi. (Pours coffee. Sits down.)

Jody: May I help you?

Teacher: No. I just came to see you.

Jody: I'm sorry. I have a lot to do right now. I don't have time to visit.

Teacher: Oh, I'm sorry. Well, how are things at home? Tell me about your kids.

"Mark," I said, "people don't hear my boundaries."

"Then you need to be more tenacious."

"What am I supposed to do? Treat them like I do children — take their little chins in my hands, plant my face in front of theirs, and say firmly, "You may be quiet."

"Whatever works for you, Jody."

Lord, help me to hold on to things with a loose grip.
Help me to see Your hand in everything I do.
Make me a vessel filled with You and emptied of myself.
Help me make good little decisions
as well as the big ones.
Let me experience being fully alive
as I yield to Your Spirit, Your way in Your time.

"Now listen, you who say, 'Today or tomorrow we will go to this or that city, spend a year there, carry on business and make money.' Why, you do not even know what will happen tomorrow. What is your life? You are a mist that appears for a little while and then vanishes. Instead, you ought to say, 'If it is the Lord's will, we will live and do this or that' " (James 14:13-15).

Hooked on Books

Who gives a good book gives more than cloth, paper and ink . . . more than leather, parchment and words. He reveals a foreword of his thoughts, a dedication of his friendship, a page of his presence, a chapter of himself and an index of his love.

—William Arthur Ward

For the first decade of my life, I was the only girl among four boys. My cousin, JoAnn, having three brothers, empathized. Our two families often spent Sunday dinners, holidays, and summers together. While the boys played ball, hunted down more frogs, and generally looked for ways to be obnoxious, we girls retreated to the bedroom with our best friends—*books*. Whenever we got together, we read for hours. Our primary memories of each other during those growing up years revolve around the world of books.

When we became adults, we moved to different areas of the country and our paths rarely crossed. But last spring I spoke in her area and we got together for the first time *alone* in twenty years. Our mutual passion had remained unchanged—it was still books. She had become a fiction writer and I, a nonfiction author. Books still brought a mutual bond.

What worlds of wealth we both have in our books. Now, let me clarify—the wealth consists not in all the money we make from sales, but rather in the richness of information and insight gained through reading.

America is producing a generation of nonreaders. This bothers me. I read to my children nightly and require that they read independently as well. They see their parents read daily. Yet they do not share my passion for reading. I blame part of this on television. Even though Paul and I limit the television time in our home to one hour a day max, the tube has still left its mark on our children. Sometimes I fantasize about our country having a major power shortage so people have to go back to spending time reading and interacting with one another instead of living their lives around the TV schedule. This includes Nintendo and video games as well. It seems as though everything has to flash and zing to catch the interest of today's children.

JoAnn and I often reflect on where we would or would not be today if our lives had been devoid of books. I find it ironic that at a time when our world has an abundance of reading material, we are producing a generation of nonreaders. At a time when we have more books on the Bible than ever, we are producing a generation of Bible illiterates.

Modern researchers have documented a connection between leadership and reading. I do believe readers are leaders. Apparently people with vision have in common the continual intake of information, much of it through the written page. But this is no new observation. George Crabbe, in the early nineteenth century, wrote the following in his work titled, *The Library:*

> This, books can do—nor this alone: they give
> New views to life, and teach us how to live;
> They soothe the grieved, the stubborn they chastise;
> Fools they admonish, and confirm the wise.
> Their aid they yield to all: they never shun

The man of sorrow, nor the wretch undone;
Unlike the hard, the selfish, and the proud,
They fly not sullen from the suppliant crowd;
Nor tell to various people various things,
But show to subjects, what they show to kings.

If you're not already in the habit, why not start reading
now? In the space below, make a list of the books you plan
to read in the next few months.

Grace's
Seal of
Approval

*G*race Bible Church. Appropriately named. God has used this group of people to provide ample evidence of His grace toward me. From the beginning, I have sensed a canopy of grace over this relationship. As a relatively new Christian (compared to all these people who seemed to get saved when they were five) I didn't expect to find acceptance. But I did. God's love in that church overflowed to me.

When someone first suggested that we send a proposal to Grace to move the school there, someone else advised, "Don't. They had a school once and have turned down every school since. . . ." I almost didn't send them a proposal, but I felt God nudging. They did accept us, which surprised everyone, including them.

I am deeply grateful to Pastor Bill Bryan for his loving warmth which welcomed me to the church. His forgiving spirit when I told him about "my terrible past" healed the hurts and fears in my heart. I cherish the precious friendship I share with Bill and Shirley.

Bill went on to be the chaplain at Dallas Theological Seminary and when a new senior pastor came, I thought the "honeymoon" was over, but it was just beginning. Two years later, when he offered me a position as Director of Children's Ministries, I nearly fainted. In fact, I turned it down. I did not want my past to come up and hurt this wonderful, highly respected conservative organization. When I prayed about it, no one felt more surprised than I to sense God's leading in this area. I took the job and loved it.

I have always appreciated Dr. Michael Fisher for bringing me into the world of Christian education. It has blessed me and opened doors for me to venture into other areas of Christian service, such as writing for a conservative publishing company, Victor Books. I could see the Lord's hand of leading and, again, the evidence of His grace.

After four years, I resigned only because I was not the Bionic Christian Woman. My load of juggling family, traveling, speaking, and writing books was too much to do while holding down a church job. But after a few months, I really missed it. Grace had hired someone and I began to receive offers from other churches.

I felt privileged to work with Dr. Gary Inrig as a consultant during this interim time. I realized how much I loved church work. After two years, I went back on staff at Grace. I decided that if God wanted me back in church work, it made most sense to go back to where our family felt most fulfilled. Frankly, after working for a much larger church in the interim, I thought going back would be really easy. Typical of how God makes us grow, the job itself has been easy, but God added a few surprises.

First, we decided to build a Children's Christian Education building. Then we had a fire. Next came a new adult building and a major event each month like VBS, Open House Dedication, Fall Festival, Holiday Bazaar, and a five-day "Joy of Sharing Christmas" musical with drama and food for the community to enjoy. But again, God's canopy of Grace has been ever evident.

When I try and do things in my flesh and energy, I grow weary. When I do God's work in HIS Spirit, I find renewal. I thank God for the opportunity to give back in a small way the abundant grace I have received from this church and its people. Psalm 119:105 says: "Your Word is a lamp to my feet and a light for my path." If you've ever used a lantern or flashlight to light your path at night, you know it only illuminates one or two steps at a time. I think about this when I reflect on God's leading, one little step at a time, in my service at Grace, both in the school and the church. It's a good thing. If He showed us the "big picture" all at once, we'd either cower in fear at the "lions, tigers and bears" (oh, my!) that lie ahead, or we'd die the slow death of anticipation over having to wait for all the great things He has planned for us!

Faithful
Friends
and
Kindred
Spirits

*G*od has blessed me with friends, kindred spirits, with whom I enjoy close, honest, long-term relationships. We have little time for going out to lunch or chatting on the phone; yet the closeness remains, transcending time and space. Why? Because it is a bond of the spirit. One look in the eyes says it all. For example, Shirley Bryan and I can have entire conversations from across crowded sanctuaries, just with our eyes. Our Swedish souls are knit together as one.

These rare jewels grow more valuable each year. As we watch each other go through the seasons of life, we realize increasingly the uniqueness of what we share, and we recognize that it is also eternal. With a kindred spirit, it doesn't matter if your best foot is forward. You don't have to censor what comes out of your mouth; you simply communicate what is on your heart and mind.

My life and schedule are so full that my family, church, and work take up nearly all my time. I have no time for superficial relationships. When I take time to be with a friend, I want to be "there," connected and authentic.

They bless my life. Spiritually they pray for me and renew my spirit. Intellectually they challenge me. Emotional ly they love unconditionally and provide abundant acceptance; and physically, they are a hug away. In Colossians 2:2, Paul refers to the goal—of hearts knit together in love. I love the image of the Lord Jesus as the heavenly handicrafter, finger-knitting two hearts into one beautiful friendship that glorifies His Father. It certainly explains the supernatural delight that elevates these friendships. As Ecclesiastes 4:12 says, "A cord of three strands is not quickly broken," and a three-way bond of two friends and Jesus in one of the most richly satisfying blessings in life.

Velveteen Rabbits

n emcee at a conference introduced the speaker, saying, "She is a wife, mother of three children ages nineteen, thirteen, and nine, and has taught for twenty-five years. She was a principal for fifteen years, has served as a Director of Christian Education for more than six years, has authored five books, and has three more coming out next year. . . ."

I looked around to see who this incredible person was, and then I heard my name. When I look out and see the glazed look in everyone's eyes, I want to say, "That's not the *real* me. Look at me. See the real me. I am not what I sound like I am. I am insecure. I am hurting. I'm vulnerable just like you." In fact, I often say I have the gift of spiritual encouragement—I encourage others by making them glad they're not me.

I'm a real Karla Klutz. My husband calls me Norma Crosby because I sometimes mispronounce words just a little. Do you ever say nucular when you mean nuclear? Or Febuary when you mean February? When our friends redecorated, I said they redid their living room in French Provisional furniture. I say stuff like, "We have a little levity in the salary," when I mean "leverage." Sometimes I wonder to myself, "Did I ask my accountant when the physical year ended when I meant fiscal?" When I speak publicly, I'm paranoid that I'll use nonexistent words like "irregardless" and "empathetic." Or I wring my hands, anxious that I'll say something wordy like "positive mental attitude" instead of just "positive attitude."

Some days the only thing holy about me is the hole in my hemline where the thread ripped out when I caught my heel in it. I am not who that introduction sounds like I really am. Therefore, my favorite kind of people are those who are "real." I appreciate people like my friend Donna who have worked through painful past experiences to be a "real" servant for Jesus Christ. "Real" friends see beyond outward appearances to what is inside of a person.

I love the story of *The Velveteen Rabbit*. Sue Bohlin, my dear friend, prayer partner, and soul friend, did a calligraphy of my favorite part of the book, which I display proudly in my office. When I feel old, tired, and unattractive, I look at Sue's gift:

"What is REAL?" asked the Rabbit one day, when they were lying side by side near the nursery fender, before Nana came to tidy the room. "Does it mean having things that buzz inside you and a stick-out handle?"

"Real isn't how you are made," said the Skin Horse. "It's a thing that happens to you. When a child loves you for a long, long time, not just to play with, but REALLY loves you, then you become Real."

"Does it hurt?" asked the Rabbit.

"Sometimes," said the Skin Horse, for he was always truthful. "When you are Real, you don't mind being hurt."

"Does it happen all at once, like being wound up," he asked, "or bit by bit?"

"It doesn't happen all at once," said the Skin Horse.

"You become. It takes a long time. That's why it doesn't often happen to people who break easily, or have sharp edges, or who have to be carefully kept. Generally, by the time you are Real, most of your hair has been loved off, and your eyes drop out and you get loose in the joints and very shabby. But these things don't matter at all, because once you are Real you can't be ugly, except to people who don't understand."

"I suppose you are Real?" said the Rabbit. And then he wished he had not said it, for he thought the Skin Horse might be sensitive. But the Skin Horse only smiled.

"The Boy's uncle made me Real," he said. "That was a great many years ago; but once you are Real you can't become unreal again. It lasts for always."*

I have said that I would rather wear out than rust out. I want God to use me to build His kingdom. But that path is not glamorous. It involves long hours, often doing thankless, unseen tasks, setting up and cleaning up after multitudes of meetings, listening, being available, being misunderstood, serving, and just getting worn out. It means sometimes feeling like you've had the effectiveness of Chuck E. Cheese instead of Chuck Colson. And it means dealing graciously with people who expect you to do the job of Jesus, Paul, and Charles Swindoll on Mother Teresa's salary. Yes, when you commit yourself to serving others in love, which is the true essence of leadership, you become shabby. But you also become real.

"Let us not become weary in doing good, for at the proper time we will reap a harvest if we do not give up. Therefore, as we have opportunity, let us do good to all people, especially to those who belong to the family of believers" (Gal. 6:9-10).

The Velveteen Rabbit or How Toys Become Real, by Margery Williams, Running Press, 1981.